Social Work and
Social Change
in Canada

Social Work and Social Change in Canada

edited by

Brian Wharf

M&S

Canadian Cataloguing in Publication Data

Main entry under title:

Social work and social change in Canada

Includes bibliographical references.
ISBN 0-7710-8799-3

1. Social service – Canada.   2. Social movements – Canada.   3. Social work education – Canada.
I. Wharf, Brian.

HV105.S63 1990   361.971   C90-094169-3

McClelland & Stewart Inc.
The Canadian Publishers
481 University Avenue
Toronto, Ontario
M5G 2E9

Printed and bound in Canada

Contents

Preface

For most of my career in social work I have been intrigued with the struggle to address private troubles and public issues in the day-to-day practice of social work. The history of the profession reveals that most of the time and attention has been directed toward private troubles, yet public issues have a demonstrable impact on the lives of the clients of social welfare agencies. Providing effective services to clients requires that at the very least social workers should document this impact, and in so doing lay the groundwork for improved social policies and programs. This argument assumes that social workers and those in charge of social policy are committed to providing effective service and to eliminating the social problems of poverty and poor housing. As will become evident in the following pages, it is by no means clear whether social workers and policy-makers in Canada have made such a commitment. Nevertheless, the authors of this book believe that social workers should address public issues, and it is our hope that the book will provoke debate on how to accomplish this objective.

This has not been an easy book to write. It was initiated some five years ago by Ben Carniol and myself on the assumption that a small group of like-minded social work educators could tackle the public issue agenda of social work without much difficulty. We chose to address this agenda through the vehicle of social movements and invited the other authors to take part in the project. It became evident fairly quickly that the initial assumption was incorrect even to the degree of like-mindedness that prevailed. All chapters have been revised several times on the basis of reviews by the authors and as a consequence of a day-long meeting held in Windsor in 1988. The comments by the anonymous reviewers selected by McClelland & Stewart were extremely useful and necessitated further revisions.

As the editor I would like to thank Roland, Yvonne, Harvey, Ben, and Joan for sticking with this project during its very difficult gestation period. Michael Harrison of McClelland & Stewart contributed many helpful comments and we are grateful for his support during the past five years. Richard Tallman did a superb job of editing a manuscript that came to him in a somewhat scrambled form and Carol Gamey constructed the index and bibliography.

Finally, I wish to acknowledge my debt to my secretary, Jean Holder, whose ability to translate my hieroglyphics into type is legendary in the Faculty of Human and Social Development.

B.W.
Victoria, B.C.
June, 1990

CHAPTER 1

Introduction

by Brian Wharf

Perhaps more so than any other human service profession, social work has sought to intervene with respect to both private troubles and public issues. The distinction between "the private troubles of milieu" and the "public issues of social structure" was developed by C. Wright Mills.

> Troubles occur within the character of the individual and within the range of his immediate relations with others; they have to do with his self and with those limited areas of social life of which he is directly and personally aware. Accordingly, the statement and the resolution of troubles properly lie within the individual as a biographical entity and within the scope of his immediate milieu - the social setting that is directly open to his personal experience and to some extent his willful activity. A trouble is a private matter: values cherished by an individual are felt by him to be threatened.
> Issues have to do with matters that transcend these local environments of the individual and the range of his inner

life. They have to do with the organization of many such milieux into the institutions of an historical society as a whole, with the ways in which various milieux overlap and interpenetrate to form the larger structure of social and historical life. An issue is a public matter: some value cherished by publics is felt to be threatened.[1]

The search for a reasonable balance between private troubles and public issues has pushed the profession to discover integrating concepts and organizational structures that would permit attention to both. In part this search by social work has also been a reflection of a larger societal debate around the central issue of the causes and the appropriate responses to private troubles and public issues. That both exist is not a matter for debate. What is and has proven difficult to resolve is the question of who should attend to public issues. Is this an appropriate responsibility for social work or should this and other human service professions concentrate energies on private troubles? Should changing social structures be left to provincial and federal governments? Alternatively, does it not make sense to take advantage of the knowledge and insights obtained by social workers about the contribution of public issues to personal troubles? How can this contribution be realized, particularly when the time and energy of social workers is consumed by private troubles, and when politicians often resent what they deem to be unwarranted intrusions into the political domain.

An important connection between the individual level and the societal level is the "immediate milieu – the social setting that is directly open to his personal experience and to some extent his willful activity." The immediate milieu refers most directly to families but includes communities of residence or of interest. Community settings provide a middle-range location for aggregating personal troubles to the level of a group or community. Consider the case of unemployment, one of the examples used by Mills.

When, in a city of 100,000, only one man is unemployed, that is his personal trouble, and for its relief we properly look to the character of the man, his skills, and his immediate opportunities. But when in a nation of 50 million employees, 15 million men are unemployed, that is an issue, and we may not hope to find its solution within the range of opportunities open to any one individual. The very structure of opportunities has collapsed.[2]

It is patently impossible for one unemployed individual or indeed a group to change the structure of opportunities at the societal level. However, a group or community can take collective action. As Carniol notes in Chapter 5, they can begin by refusing to accept the responsibility for structural employment and can act on this position, both by organizing demonstrations of protest and by pursuing the strategy of community economic development. The reframing of personal troubles into a group or community concern leads to a middle-range strategy that is particularly appropriate for social work given its long-standing involvement in community organization.

While there have been many attempts to grapple with the fusion of public issues and private troubles this book differs from previous attempts in three significant ways. The first distinguishing characteristic is the connection to social movements. Social movements have been defined as "socially shared activities and beliefs directed toward the demand for social change in some aspect of the social order."[3] Since social movements address public issues, the present book reviews the experience of three social movements to determine whether social work can learn from their experience. The movements selected for study are the women's, labour, and First Nation movements. To our knowledge no other attempt to connect personal troubles and public issues has done so by inquiring into the applicability of the lessons learned from social movements for social work.

The second identifying characteristic of the book lies in the assertion that the challenge of addressing public issues and private troubles can be accomplished only if public issues are included at the very core of the day-to-day practice of front-line social workers. The rationale for this position is that the vast majority of social workers are engaged in direct practice and only if a concern for public issues is built into their practice will these be addressed.

The third characteristic is to consider whether communities of residence or of interest can provide a middle ground for dealing with public issues. Such a middle-range strategy may appropriately deal with some public issues and may afford a platform for changing structures and policies at the societal level. Since social workers have been involved in community work for many years, focusing on this level of practice may be both feasible and appropriate.

Given that this book is intended for social work students and given the relative paucity of information available to these students about social movements, a principal objective is to present information about three significant social movements in Canada. The accounts of these social movements are organized around two central questions.

(1) Can social work profit from the experience of social movements? For example, can feminist theory inform and guide social work practice? Can organizing social workers into unions bring pressure to bear on agencies and on governments to provide increased benefits for clients? Does the approach to social work practice being developed in First Nation communities address public issues and private troubles?

(2) If there are lessons to be learned from social movements, can some changes in social work education and practice be suggested? If so, are changes in the policies and structures of social welfare agencies required?

The book is organized in the following fashion. This introductory chapter sets the stage by outlining the historical concern of social work for public issues and social problems. Chapter 2 outlines the attempt of the Carleton School of Social Work to develop a curriculum that addresses both public issues and private troubles. Chapters 3, 4, and 5 consider the questions outlined above and in so doing inquire into the connections between the day-to-day practice of social work and the social movements of women, First Nations, and labour. The task of summarizing the lessons from social movements and the implications for social work education and practice is addressed in the concluding chapter.

It should be emphasized at the outset that the authors of the case studies found few connections between social work practice and social movements. This is most pronounced in the case of Chapter 4. While aware of some emerging connections, Yvonne Howse and Harvey Stalwick deemed these to be minor when compared to the well-intentioned but damaging interventions of social workers into the lives of Indian families. Faced with this record, Howse and Stalwick focus their study on past relationships between social workers and Indian people and emphasize that Indian people have to recognize and name their oppressors, including social workers, before connections can be made. Hence, Chapter 4 does not respond to the questions outlined above. Instead, it tells a story of oppression and conceptualizes this story through the framework provided by writers such as Freire.[4]

Chapters 3 and 5 address the questions in a more direct fashion. Yet even with the women's and labour movements it proved to be difficult to identify close connections between these movements and social work. As will become evident in the following pages, the agenda within social work calling for change has slipped away, leaving the action to social movements and other groups. For this reason alone the case studies make compelling reading for social workers and social work students interested in social change. While connections may be few at the present time, these studies may stimulate debate among students and practitioners as to how connections might be established in the future. Indeed, an explicit objective of this book is to provoke discussion within the profession on its commitment to social change.

Before proceeding to the discussion on private troubles and public issues it is necessary to devote some time to semantics. Such terms as "social change," "social reform," "structural change," and "societal change" are frequently used interchangeably, but to some these terms have quite precise meanings. Because of the variations in meaning it is necessary to indicate how these terms are used in this book. "Social reform" typically refers to improving or altering existing policies and legislation without, however, changing the basic structures of Canadian society. By contrast, the terms "societal change" and "structural change" are concerned with creating fundamental changes in Canadian society by finding alternatives to or drastically altering representative democracy and the free enterprise economy. Finally, "social change" is used here as an umbrella term encompassing both social reform and structural change.

The Struggle to Connect Private Troubles and Public Issues

It is impossible in the confines of a brief introductory chapter to trace in detail all of the efforts that have been made to integrate public issues and private troubles at both theoretical and practical levels. The reader is referred to writings by the early theorists and architects of the profession, such as Mary Richmond and Bertha Reynolds,[5] and to historical reviews by Roy Lubove and Clarke Chambers.[6] These are American authors and they present information about the early days of social work in the United States. Canadian social work education and theory have been largely borrowed from the U.S., but it is nonetheless striking to recognize that none of the early or current theorists who have sought to develop unifying constructs are Canadian. Richmond, Schwartz, Pincus and Minahan, and Germain and Gitterman, to name only the best-known integrators, are all American.[7] One is left with the disturbing question as to the fit between U.S. theory and Canadian practice, both in earlier years and at the present time. The fit or lack of fit is explored in a later section of this chapter and again in the final chapter.

Nevertheless, given the extent to which social work theory and education have been derived from the U.S., it is useful to review briefly some of the attempts to connect private troubles and public issues. Mary Richmond is widely regarded as a principal architect of the social work profession. Her writings in the 1920s represent one approach to fusing public issues and private troubles. For Richmond the unique contribution of social work was knowledge of the individual and of the individual's social environment.

> In *Social Diagnosis* and *What is Social Casework?* Mary Richmond attempted to explain the unity of social work despite practice in a variety of institutions or agency settings. It applied to problems of human maladjustment a differential casework, based upon the accumulation and interpretation of social evidence. Social evidence was a unique form of insight into the human personality, different from that of the psychiatrist, psychologist, or any other group concerned with human relations.[8]

This unique contribution was affirmed by an early friend of social work, Dr. Richard Cabot, who was largely responsible for introducing social work to hospitals.

> In extending services to individuals who required more than straightforward medical advice, the hospital caseworker helped socialize her institution; and the facts she accumulated in daily work shed light on the social origins of disease – housing, living and working conditions. From the beginning, Dr. Cabot hoped that medical social work would contribute to the development of preventive medicine. Through casework the community could better understand and control the environmental conditions which undermined health and delayed the recovery of the sick.[9]

These early conceptualizations emphasized the importance of understanding and changing the social environment of clients. Social work practice based on these conceptualizations found an appropriate agency environment in the settlement houses. Perhaps the most famous settlement house in the United States was Hull House in Chicago, founded by Jane Addams in 1889. Others, such as Henry Street Settlement in New York, were established in later years, mainly in large cities on the eastern seaboard. The settlement houses are important to this discussion for two reasons. First, their location in inner-city neighbourhoods meant that staff became intimately aware of local needs and problems and developed programs to meet these needs.

Second, these local efforts pushed them to involvement in nation-wide social reforms to alleviate poverty and to protect children. Evelyn Burns notes, "What made the great leaders of the past so influential was their commitment to a cause. They cared desperately about people, they had a vision of the good life and they were morally indignant about social evil."[10]

Similarly, Kramer and Specht describe the contribution of settlement houses on social reform in the following terms:

> The settlement houses, a second important social movement of the early part of the century, based many of their programs on social action to promote social legislation. Whereas the Charity Organization movement represented the community's attempt to help individuals adjust to social situations by the use of scientific helping processes, the settlement movement represented the community's desire to change society to meet people's needs. The reformers of the settlements, namely, Jane Addams, Lillian Wald, and Florence Kelly, developed techniques for promoting social legislation and political action to achieve change. Workmen's Compensation laws, the White House Conference on Children, child labour laws, the establishment of the Children's Bureau, and some of the social experiments of the New Deal can be attributed in part to the actions and the spirit of the settlement movements.[11]

It is important to note that social reformers like Jane Addams, Florence Kelly, and Grace and Earl Abbott "made an impact because they had influence in the right places at the right time on that small remnant of the citizenry that was both concerned and powerful."[12] Typically, this citizenry consisted of young politicians who were concerned with social conditions and who argued the case for reform as an integral part of of their platform to gain power.

Settlement houses were private organizations governed by elected boards of citizens and supported through philanthropic sources. Some exist today and still provide appropriate auspices for attending to private troubles and community concerns. But the partnership between aspiring politicians like Robert Wagner and Franklin Delano Roosevelt and settlement house leaders has disappeared, and with it the capacity to engage in reforms to alter national policies.

The early years of social work in the United States were well suited to integrating private troubles and public issues. While the settlement houses provided the most congenial environment, other agencies such as hospitals and psychiatric clinics welcomed the contribution of social workers, who provided information about the social environment and who knew about and could mobilize community resources. But the uniqueness of this contribution was to be short-lived. Stung by the criticism of Abraham Flexner in 1915 that social work did not possess a distinctive body of knowledge (as Lubove notes, "apparently Flexner did not consider the possibility that liaison and resource mobilization in a complex urban society was a professional function requiring considerable skill and specialized learning"),[13] social workers increasingly deserted the social environment and social reform functions in favour of a focus on individuals. Crudely put, mucking about in the environment came to be seen as neither as professional nor as scientific as clinical skills in relationship and behavioural therapy. This latter thrust was given a considerable boost by the psychological insights into behaviour provided by Freud and his followers. Social work, like psychiatry and psychology, was quick to incorporate these insights into both education and practice.

The historian Lubove is not tentative in his assertion that central to any understanding of social work's development as a profession is the manner in which caseworkers established themselves as the spokespeople for social work's professional aspiration. In addition, schools of social work "played no small role in elevating casework to the nuclear skill in social work."[14] Indeed, Virginia Robinson claimed that social work came of age in the 1920s when its focus shifted from the environment to the psyche of individuals.[15] With the abandonment of the environment and of social reform and the emergence of social casework as the dominant force in the profession, it is no wonder that for the next thirty years the profession came to be identified with clinical helping skills.

This sketchy review of the search for integrating concepts in the early years of social work in the U.S. requires some additional comments. First, the reform initiatives in the late nineteenth century to protect children from abuse at home and in factories gradually resulted in the development of societies to prevent cruelty to children. For example, the Toronto Humane Society was established in 1887. Subsequently, the public issue of unemployment forced itself onto the consciousness of the U.S. and Canada during the depression, and state and local agencies were then created to provide financial assistance to the unemployed. These agencies required staff to carry out the functions of determining eligibility for financial assistance and investigating conditions of child neglect. The staff of both relief and child protection agencies were called social workers but even today the majority lack professional training. More importantly, the refusal of the federal and provincial governments to fund these programs adequately has meant that staff must attend to never-ending crises. Chronic underfunding has thwarted the efforts of social workers to be caring and compassionate, let alone to be clinical therapists. Hence, for most social workers in public and child welfare agencies, the theoretical formulations of psychoanalytic and functional casework have had little relevance whereas the integrated approach of Richmond and Reynolds and others might have been useful both for clients and workers. It would at least have allowed social workers to attend to personal troubles within the context of their local environment.

Second, the dominance of social casework and its unrelenting focus on personal troubles were responsible for the emergence of two other specialized methods – group work and community organization. The interest in this book is in the latter specialization, which had its origins in the charity organization movement in the early years of this century. The charity organization movement stressed the need for co-ordination to avoid duplication between agencies. This agenda of co-ordinating agency efforts remains an elusive and unfulfilled objective even today. The Lane Report of 1939, which represented a milestone in the development of community organization, defined community organization as "(a) the discovery and definition of needs, (b) the elimination and prevention of social needs and disabilities as far as possible, and (c) the articulation of resources and needs and the constant readjustment of resources in order to better meet changing needs."[16]

The early years of community organization practice were heavily influenced by Murray Ross. To this day Ross's book, *Community Organization*, remains the only Canadian text to have enjoyed widespread use as a basic text in U.S. schools of social work.[17] For Ross, community organization was dedicated to the task of assisting neighbourhoods to develop the capacity to look after their own affairs, and indeed this enabling approach dominated the practice of community organization for many years. By 1970 other approaches had emerged. In his now classic article, Jack Rothman described and distinguished among three approaches to community organization. Rothman gave the label "locality development" to the community organization approach described by Ross, and then identified the social planning and social action approaches. Social planning "emphasizes a technical process of problem-solving with regard to substantive social problems. . . Rational deliberately planned and controlled change has a central part in this model." By contrast, social action "seeks redistribution of power, resources or decision-making in the community and on changing basic policies of formal organizations."[18]

The post-war years in Canada were characterized by specialization in the methods of casework, group work, and community organization. Interest in uniting private troubles and public issues waned until the 1960s, when it re-emerged for a number of reasons. However, before exploring the more recent attempts at integration it is necessary to give some attention to the early years of Canadian social work and social reform.

The Early Years in Canadian Social Work

The definitive history of the development of social work in Canada has yet to be written. Indeed, one of the few articles available asserts that "Two movements, the charity organization societies and the settlement movement, were of particular significance in the development of social work."[19] From the perspective of the U.S. this is an accurate statement, since both charity organization societies and settlement houses flourished in this country. However, neither was a significant force in Canada. Whatever the legacy of these movements has been for social work in the U.S., and it has been argued here that settlement houses offered particularly appropriate auspices to address private troubles and public issues, this legacy does not exist in Canada.

According to Guest, social reforms in Canada in the late nineteenth and early twentieth centuries were spearheaded by the urban reform movement, the Social Gospel movement, and muckraking journalists. Guest gives particular attention to the pioneering work of Herbert Ames, J.J. Kelso, and J.S. Woodsworth. Ames was a wealthy businessman who undertook a survey of the housing and other social conditions of residents of a working-class district in Montreal in 1896. "Ames helped Canadians to redefine the causes of poverty. His research demonstrated that the problem was largely rooted in economic and social arrangements."[20]

The crusading journalist J.J. Kelso investigated the plight of abused and neglected children in Toronto. Kelso became so committed to the cause of reform that he established the Toronto Humane Society, campaigned for legislation to protect children, and subsequently became the first president of the Toronto Children's Aid Society.

J.S. Woodsworth began his distinguished career as a Methodist minister and in this capacity was appointed superintendent of the People's Mission in Winnipeg. Woodsworth then became the secretary of the Canadian Welfare League. "The purpose of the league was to promote a general interest in all forms of social welfare."[21] Woodsworth also organized the first university-based training program in social work in 1915.

These men and other early social reformers, such as Nellie McClung and Agnes Macphail, who fought for the rights of women, were identified as social workers. As a result of their efforts, state or state-supported agencies were developed to protect children and assist the poor. However, the staff hired by these agencies were unable to carry on the tradition of reform. They were hobbled both by the demands of day-to-day practice and by the fact that employment by the state prohibited them from engaging in reform activities. In a very real sense, these constraints have continued to the present day. Except for a few notable exceptions in cities such as Vancouver, Winnipeg, and Toronto, the settlement house movement did not become a significant force in the social welfare scene in Canada. Lacking such appropriate auspices, and contrary to the experience in the United States, most of the early social workers in Canada were not social reformers, nor were they imbued with Richmond's sense of the importance of the environment.

Nevertheless, a handful of Canadian social workers continued the Woodsworth tradition of social reform. Charlotte Whitton, Harry Cassidy, and Leonard Marsh were the architects of much of the existing social security system in Canada. Their reform efforts were continued by deputy ministers and other senior officials in the federal Department of Health and Welfare. Senior civil servants such as George Davidson and Joe Willard were committed to developing a comprehensive national social security program, although they were unable to realize their vision in its entirety. However, in recent years the provincial and federal governments have sought to cut back on social welfare programs in order to reduce provincial and federal debts. While not expressed in the same forthright way as in the U.K., where Prime Minister Thatcher views social and health programs as a problem to be eliminated, the social policy agenda in Canada is directed toward reducing health and social programs.

Hence, the mantle of leadership for progressive social policy is no longer assumed by government, and this requires that the social work profession, social movements, and voluntary organizations become more vigorous and committed to social change. A number of organizations – the Canadian Association of Social Workers, the Canadian Council on Social Development, the National Council of Welfare, the National Anti-Poverty Organization, the National Action Committee on the Status of Women, and the National Pensioners and Senior Citizens Federation – have formed the Social Policy Reform group. This coalition has represented the cause of the poor and low-income earners and has sought to change the tax and the income security systems. Nevertheless, it is apparent that these organizations seek to reform existing arrangements rather than force fundamental change in the social order.

From Generalist to Ecological Practice: Can Ecological Theory Address Public Issues?

For a variety of reasons, including the decline of community organization as a field of specialization in social work education and practice and the development of undergraduate programs in social work education, interest in general practice re-emerged in the 1970s. From this interest flowed theories about generalist practice that attempted to strike a new balance between emphasis on individuals and on environments.

These fresh attempts built on the work of theorists such as William Schwartz, who conceptualized social work as primarily having a mediation role, serving as broker between the individual and social groups.[22] Others elaborated on this approach by incorporating systems theory into social work and using this theory as a bridge between individuals and their environment. Thus the authors of a frequently used book in social work practice stated: "Social work is concerned with the interactions between people and their social environments which affect the ability of people to accomplish their life tasks, alleviate distress and realize their aspirations and values."[23] According to systems theory, various social systems, such as families, employment, schools, and social agencies, have common characteristics. These common features include each system having its own boundaries, its own subsystems, and interactions with other systems as well as with individuals. Though these systems are generally understood as offering positive environments for individuals, systems theory acknowledges that some systems may be inadequate or, indeed, harmful.

A recent elaboration of systems theory is the ecological approach to social work, which has been articulated by a number of writers, including Ann Hartman and Joan Laird in their *Family-Centered Social Work Practice*:

> We have learned that all living things are dependent for survival on nurturant and sustaining environments and that they are interdependent on each other. . . . An ecological orientation dictates that the individual cannot be understood outside the context of the intimate environment; the family can be understood only in the context of the larger environment.[24]

The ecological approach seems progressive and has found favour among social work educators because it promises to bring about change not only in individuals but also in social conditions. This is indicated by Germain and Gitterman in *Life Model of Social Work Practice*:

> The social worker's professional function is to help people use their adaptive and coping capacities to obtain available and accessible environmental resources. When such resources are missing, inaccessible, withheld or denied, the professional function is to influence those structures and processes to be more responsive to client need.[25]

Such textbooks present examples of how social workers can remove communication barriers between a client and organizations such as schools, hospitals, and housing authorities. They also offer illustrations of workers advocating for increased benefits for clients. However, these examples and the practical frameworks are too often limited to changes for particular clients in particular situations. The task of improving the environment for all clients by increasing income benefits and improving housing conditions has proven to be largely impervious to the efforts of social workers.

Despite the current popularity and attractiveness of ecological and systems theories, the argument developed in this book is that they do not provide an adequate explanation of change and how it occurs. First, from a theoretical point of view, an inherent weakness in systems theory is the assumption that problems, once identified, will generate a demand for change, and that change will then occur and the problem will be solved. This assumption ignores the capacity of Canadian society to tolerate many problems (poverty, child neglect and violence against women, the unequal distribution of wealth, and the devaluation of minority cultures) on a continuing basis.

A second weakness of ecological theory is that it ignores power and its distribution in Canada. Thus the fit between the person and his/her environment for the rich and the upper middle classes is comfortable, but it is not so for the poor or low-income earners. However, changing the environment to increase the fit for the poor is extremely difficult since those for whom the fit is fine also exercise a disproportionate amount of power in Canadian society. While first viewed as radical and perhaps biased and unscientific, the analyses of power and how it works in Canada by scholars such as Porter (1965), Clement (1975 and 1983), and Panitch (1977) are now largely accepted as accurate.[26] These analyses have consistently revealed the extent to which a relatively small group of businessmen control Canadian industry and through their positions as captains of industry exercise a disproportionate amount of power in the political life of Canada. The analyses have further demonstrated that business leaders, politicians, and senior bureaucrats have much in common in terms of values and lifestyles. They tend to view society, its issues, and its problems in a very similar fashion. Hence, despite the existence of representative democracy, Canada is ruled by an elite group of leaders holding positions of power in business and in politics.

Flowing from the above, the basic philosophical position of the contributors to this book is described in Chapter 3 by Joan Gilroy as follows: "In contrast to the predominant view of governments as impartial, radical scholars show them to be aligned with the interests of the powerful and to act rather consistently to support these interests."

A third weakness is that social workers and other human service professionals have not been assigned the responsibility for bringing about changes at the societal level or even within communities. Placing these responsibilities on social workers immediately leads to the charge of meddling in politics – the preserve of politicians, not professionals. It is safer and easier for social workers – indeed, for all human service professionals – to restrict their care and attention to people already experiencing problems rather than to draw attention to conditions that in large measure cause these problems. The boundaries between political and community action, between politicians and professionals who push for change, and between politicians and special interest groups have never been clear.

The final weakness of ecological theory is that it does not address the issue of auspices. What kind of social welfare agency is appropriate to attend to private troubles, to modify environments at the local level, and to engage in social reform? The viability of the settlement house has been noted, as has its relative absence in Canada. Nevertheless, the issue is important because the mandate and structure of organizations that employ social workers are crucial in determining roles and responsibilities.

Ecological theory appears to assume that the practitioner is free from constraints imposed by agency auspices. Thus, ecological practitioners can change the behaviour of individuals, can alter the family or community context, and can modify the policies of agencies and governments. However, social workers are typically employed by agencies and governments, and as will become abundantly clear as the discussion in the following chapters proceeds, employment in public-sector organizations places enormous constraints on the ability of social workers to effect changes in the legislation and policies of their own or other provincial ministries. On first examination there may seem to be fewer constraints in non-governmental organizations, yet these agencies largely depend on the public purse for funds and are therefore reluctant to criticize government policies. Only very few organizations, such as sexual assault centres, other agencies serving women, and family service agencies, have accepted a dual responsibility of providing services to individuals and engaging in social reform activities.

Why Is It Necessary To Confront Public Issues?

With the formidable obstacles confronting a profession in attempts to address public issues, the question is immediately raised, Why bother? The first reason is that for most clients of social welfare agencies, the environment is one characterized by poverty, poor housing, and lack of amenities. Thus a report by the National Council of Welfare stated that "One fundamental characteristic of the child welfare system has not changed appreciably over the years: its clients are still overwhelmingly drawn from the ranks of Canada's poor."[27] More recently, major studies by the Canadian Council on Social Development, the Macdonald Royal Commission, the Nielsen Task Force, and the National Council of Welfare have all documented the extent of poverty in Canada and have drawn attention to the inadequate benefits paid in all provinces to citizens who receive social assistance. Some comments from the National Council of Welfare make the point in a convincing fashion:

3.7 million Canadians remain poor, including more than a million children under age 16 (1,016,000 in 1986) or one child in every six. Certain groups are particularly vulnerable to poverty. Over half (56.0%) of one-parent families headed by women are poor. Six in ten children being raised by a sole-support mother are poor. Four in ten unattached women (those who live alone or with non-relatives) are poor.

The "feminization of poverty" is a striking long-term trend, although it has not increased during the eighties. In 1961 13.2 percent of low-income families were headed by women; by 1986 their proportion had almost tripled to 35.1 percent. Women comprise 61.6 percent of poor unattached individuals. Females are over represented among Canada's poor: they make up 56.1 percent of all children and adults living on low incomes as opposed to 50.8 percent of the population as a whole.[28]

The feminization of poverty, the increase in single-parent families headed by women, and the high increase of poverty among Native Indians mean that women and Natives form a disproportionate share of the clients of social welfare agencies. This is, of course, the rationale for the case studies in this book focusing on women and Natives.

One crucial failure of the Canadian welfare state is its inability to provide an adequate standard of living for families who depend in part or in whole on public assistance. In all provinces, to receive social assistance is to live below the poverty line.

It must be acknowledged that there have been some very positive aspects of the welfare state in Canada. The development of universal programs such as Family Allowances and Old Age Security has not only provided benefits in a stigma-free fashion but has contributed, albeit in a modest fashion, to redistributing income from the rich to the poor. The more recent Child Tax Credit has been a significant improvement in the social security system, and despite concerns about mounting costs Canada's universal health care system is regarded as one of the best in the world.

Nevertheless the combined consequence of Canada's economic, tax, and social policies is that the rich receive a disproportionately large share of the national income.

Income is distributed in a highly unequal and regressive manner, and there has been little progress in redistributing income over the last 35 years. Families in the lowest income group have only 6.3 percent of total family income. The highest-income families, in contrast, enjoy 39.4 percent of total family income – six times the poor group's share. The distribution of income among unattached individuals is even more skewed: the top group gets 44.7 percent of total income – eight times the bottom group's 5.3 percent share.[29]

There is, then, a need to continue to push for reform in policies governing taxation, income security, and housing. And as noted above, many provincial governments and the federal government have given priority to reducing deficits rather than advancing the position of poor and low-income citizens. Leadership clearly has to be assumed by the profession of social work and by social movements.

A second reason can be found in the arguments of Mills, Richmond, Schwartz, and some ecological theorists. The problems of many clients of social welfare agencies cannot be neatly classified and separated. Clients who are unemployed and who live in poverty, besides having to cope with the crippling effects of being poor, often experience private troubles, such as parent/child and marital difficulties. These clients experience both sets of problems and they require a dual response: a personal trouble response of support, counselling, and membership in self-help groups; and a public-issue response that will change their environments at both the community and societal levels. Hence, the only effective response to people experiencing private troubles that are in large part the result of societal dysfunction is to combine all of these components – personal, community, and societal. As noted earlier, this integrated response was provided in earlier times in the U.S. by the settlement houses.

A third reason lies in the need to strengthen the agenda for change within the profession of social work. As will become evident in the following chapters, the profession has become part of the problem. Rather than being advocates for and with the poor, for the homeless and other client groups, social workers have become agents of social control, rationing inadequate benefits and services to an essentially powerless group of individuals. As Joan Gilroy notes in her chapter on the women's movement, social workers are often identified by clients as the enemy, and this perception is documented in recent texts such as *Case Critical* and *Street Level Bureaucracy*.[30]

The social work profession has grappled with this issue only hesitantly and partially, yet it has nevertheless been more involved in the struggle to combine personal troubles and public issues than any other profession. As noted at the beginning of this chapter, this book is dedicated to renewing the search. That search has included both the development of community organization and the generalist and ecological approaches to social work practice. Neither of these approaches has proven to be entirely satisfactory, and this book continues the search by examining whether any lessons can be gleaned from the experience of three social movements.

Notes

1. C.W. Mills, *The Sociological Imagination* (New York: Oxford University Press, 1959), p. 8.
2. *Ibid.*, p. 9.
3. Joseph Gusfield, *Protest, Reform and Revolt: A Reader in Social Movements* (New York: Wiley & Son, 1970), p. 2.
4. Paulo Freire, *Pedagogy of the Oppressed* (New York: Continuum Publishing, 1985).
5. See Mary Richmond, *Social Diagnosis* (New York: Russell Sage Foundation, 1930); Bertha Reynolds, "Whom Do Social Workers Serve?" *Social Work Today*, 2 (1935).
6. See Roy Lubove, *The Professional Altruist* (Cambridge, Mass.: Harvard University Press, 1965); Clarke Chambers, *The Seedtime of Reform* (Minneapolis: University of Minnesota Press, 1963).
7. Richmond, *Social Diagnosis*; William Schwartz, "Private Troubles and Public Issues: One Social Work Job or Two?" in *The Social Work Forum* (New York: Columbia University Press, 1969); Allen Pincus and Anne Minahan, *Social Work Practice: Model and Method* (Itasca, Ill.: F.E. Peacock Publishers, 1973); Carel Germain and Alex Gitterman, *The Life Model of Social Work Practice* (New York: Columbia University Press, 1980).
8. Lubove, *The Professional Altruist*, pp. 48–49.
9. *Ibid.*, p. 28.
10. Eveline Burns, "Social Welfare is our Commitment," *Public Welfare*, 16, 3 (1958), p. 153.
11. R. Kramer and H. Specht, *Readings in Community Organization Practice* (Englewood Cliffs, N.J.: Prentice-Hall, 1983), p. 3.
12. Chambers, *The Seedtime of Reform*, p. 261.
13. Lubove, *The Professional Altruist*, p. 106.
14. *Ibid.*, p. 150.
15. Virginia Robinson, "Psychiatric Social Work," *The Survey*, LII (1924).
16. Robert Lane, "The Field of Community Organization," in *Proceedings of the National Conference of Social Work* (New York: Columbia University Press, 1939).
17. Murray Ross, *Community Organization: Theory and Practice* (Toronto: Harper & Brokers, 1955).
18. Jack Rothman, "Three Models of Community Organization Practice," in F. Cox *et al.*, eds., *Strategies of Community Organization*, Second Edition (Itasca, Ill.: F.E. Peacock Publishers, 1970), p. 24.
19. Robert Chandler, "The Profession of Social Work," in Joanne and

Francis Turner, eds., *Canadian Social Welfare* (Don Mills, Ont.: Collier-Macmillan, 1986).

20. Dennis Guest, *The Emergence of Social Security in Canada* (Vancouver: University of British Columbia Press, 1980), p. 29.

21. Grace McInnis, *J.S. Woodsworth, A Man to Remember* (Toronto: Macmillan, 1953), p. 87.

22. Schwartz, "Private Troubles and Public Issues."

23. Pincus and Minahan, *Social Work Practice*.

24. Ann Hartman and Joan Laird, *Family-Centered Social Work Practice* (New York: The Free Press, 1983), pp. 69–70.

25. Germain and Gitterman, *The Life Model of Social Work Practice*, p. 141.

26. See John Porter, *The Vertical Mosaic* (Toronto: University of Toronto Press, 1965); Wallace Clement, *The Canadian Corporate Elite: An Analysis of Economic Power* (Toronto: McClelland and Stewart, 1975); Clement, *Class, Power and Property* (Toronto: Methuen, 1983); Leo Panitch, ed., *The Canadian State, Political Economy and Political Power* (Toronto: University of Toronto Press, 1977).

27. National Council of Welfare, *In the Best Interests of the Child* (Ottawa, 1979), p. 2.

28. National Council of Welfare, *Poverty Profile* (Ottawa, 1988), p. 2.

29. *Ibid.*, p. 105.

30. See Ben Carniol, *Case Critical: The Dilemma of Social Work in Canada* (Toronto: Between the Lines, 1987); Michael Lipsky, *Street Level Bureaucracy* (New York: Russell Sage Foundation, 1980).

CHAPTER 2

Connecting Private Troubles and Public Issues in Social Work Education

by Roland Lecomte

Social work history is characterized by a constant preoccupation with the dual focus on individual and social change. The difficulty that has persisted since the inception of social work as a profession is that of relating these two levels of concern. As William Schwartz points out, each generation identifies the dual focus in its own terms.[1] Mary Richmond's "wholesale" and "retail" methods, Porter Lee's "cause" and "function," and Clarke Chambers's "prophets" and "priests" identify the struggle involved in relating the "private" and the "public," the "individual" and the "social," the "personal" and the "political."[2] Many other writers, too, have emphasized the tension of the dual focus in social work. Some, including Chambers, propose choosing one over the other; others encourage maintenance and extension of the duality, placing different social work practitioners in each sphere;[3] still others place social workers outside the

31

duality, arguing that they provide a "third force," the force that mediates between the social and the individual.[4] Finally, some contributors to the debate seek to integrate the two perspectives into a single, more effective practice suggesting that the "personal *is* political" and that individual services and social action are parts of the same act.[5]

Social work education is not impervious to such dualistic pressures. Curriculum designs are often fragmented into "clinical" and "policy" tracks, "personal" intervention and "social" intervention streams, "macro" and "micro" camps, clinical practice and social action, etc. Even core courses such as Human Behaviour and the Social Environment are often split into two parts, one examining the "psychological" dimensions (sometimes taught by a psychologist) and another stressing the "social" side (usually taught by a sociologist). These approaches to therapy and practice are often developed separately, unequally, and often as adversaries. "Clinical" practitioners are accused by the "social policy" analysts of neglecting the necessity of social change, of promoting social control; "policy" workers are perceived by "clinicians" as devaluing the necessity of personal and family intervention. And the courses on Human Behaviour and the Social Environment often leave the students with simplistic psychological and sociological reductionism and determinism.

Many educators have given up the hope of resolving these issues through some form of rapprochement or integration *or* through some form of grand unitary framework.[6] They promote further specialization within each orientation and an eclectic stance in the face of proliferating theoretical and practice models currently flooding the profession. Other educators argue that these unresolved dualisms can no longer be maintained, pointing out that it is a fallacy to regard each orientation as somehow mutually exclusive. Rather, they suggest that both must be accorded equal weight in a model that should see the links as both reciprocal and dynamic.[7] The prospect for social work education lies precisely with its ability to recognize and affirm that individual and social changes are closely intertwined both in theory and in practice.

The Experience of Connecting Private Troubles and Public Issues in Social Work Education

It has been argued that the main reason for the split in the social work profession, in education and in practice, is the discipline's weddedness to individualism throughout its development. A review of the solutions offered by key social work theorists leads a renowned educator to conclude that "existing formulas to deal simultaneously with the individual and the environment, however named, are without exception, individualistic in nature."[8] Included in this critique are systems theories and ecological approaches, which had been perceived as the ones bridging the gap between the individual and the environment, between "private troubles" and "public issues."

But we are reminded that the search must go on and that the role of the educator is to translate personal troubles into public issues and public issues into the terms of their human meaning for a variety of individuals.[9] This means combining in the teaching of social work a critical awareness of the structural and historical context with the bio-psychological aspects of each individual.[10] It is not sufficient to teach "self-awareness" of one's own subjective limitations and strengths, we must also develop a critical consciousness of the objective structural forces that determine one's awareness and of how we can be empowered to act on these forces through collective action.

The translation of such lofty objectives into social work curriculum is most challenging. It has a history of struggle, disaffection, critical analysis, and creative endeavours. Shifts in philosophical, theoretical, and educational orientations are the results of personal and social circumstances. At Carleton University, the shift in orientation was a response to both pressures from without and disaffection from within. In the 1960s the socio-economic and political climate lent itself to change. Canadian society was witnessing the rise of the civil rights and anti-poverty movements, the women's movement, and student militancy. In the late 1970s and early 1980s social welfare institutions were experiencing severe cutbacks and the role and effectiveness of social workers were heavily criticized. The

School of Social Work experienced a "structural" move from St. Patrick's College (University of Ottawa) to Carleton University. This was accompanied by major changes in direction, staffing, resource allocations, and professional ideology. Within this context attempts were made by some educators, students, and practitioners to develop a progressive curriculum that would link "personal troubles" and "public issues" both in theory and in practice within a social change perspective. I wish to comment briefly on some of the issues involved in this endeavour. I hope that as in any case study, one may identify with the experience and benefit by the process.

The Development of a Progressive Curriculum

The first characteristic of a progressive curriculum is its *explicit* philosophical orientation in the analysis of social and personal problems, the analysis of the purpose of social work, the principles of social work practice, and the teaching and learning process. At Carleton, one can read in the 1988–89 university calendar:

> The Master of Social Work program is based on an analytical and critical approach to social work practice, and to knowledge related to practice. The program examines the structural context of personal and social problems, and of social work practice. The structural context refers to the interaction between the personal and the social, political, and economic aspects of such problems. The program focuses on the development of forms of practice predicated on this notion, referred to as structural approaches, seeking to intervene to change the nature of the interaction between people and their structural context. Analyses of class, gender and race relations are considered central to the program.

> Essentially, the orientation stresses that personal and social problems are perceived as manifestations of entrenched structural inequalities related to class, gender, and race that are not amenable to major change through traditional measures, and it

clearly recognizes the need for both personal and social change. This stance evolved out of an arduous and exciting endeavour.

The Search for an Organizing Framework

In the mid-1970s a group of faculty members and students, with the co-operation of many practitioners and visiting professors, undertook a thorough review of the School's curriculum. The challenge of identifying linking concepts in the course "Human Behaviour and Structural Context," for instance, led to the search for theoretical perspectives that would facilitate such an interaction. The same process occurred in the search for practice approaches that would account for *both* personal and social change. It ensured a period of exciting intellectual activities that cannot be easily characterized here. The process followed by the different groups of participants was very much related to the issues involved in the "personal" and "public" debates. Many educators and practitioners in the seventies were confronted with two relatively self-contained perspectives: one was of *personal troubles* as mostly determined by early and current individual and family experiences, and consequently the need to intervene in the individual's past and mediate experiences to allow for self-realization or personal growth; the other was of an oppressive social order that shapes human behaviour, determines one's consciousness, and leads to the experiencing of *public issues* in terms of personal troubles, and consequently the necessity to alter the oppressive social conditions through planned change and political action to allow for the individual's liberation and fulfilment.

The commitment to one or the other perspective led to much division among educators over the objectives of social work education and a plea for a critical analysis of latent and manifest ideological assumptions in the training of social workers.[11] There was a disenchantment with the vague notion of "social environment," which pervaded the social work literature. The "personal" *per se* and the family were much written about, while the social system as an entity that can shape individuals and the family within the specific historical conditions was relatively untheorized and neglected. There were simplistic assumptions that somehow personal awareness and growth could be achieved in a vacuum or that these could lead automatically to social change.

The significant concern of most people involved in the curriculum-building "collectives" at the School was the search for perspectives or frameworks that would move from a *dualistic* view of the "personal" and the "social" to a *dialectical* one. The search for such connections between the two was troublesome and is still incomplete. It is a process with both a "personal" and a "social" history. Many of us, especially those trained in the sixties, had been greatly influenced by Freudian and neo-Freudian theories. We had become uneasy with the overwhelming attention given to the influence of consciousness and the unconscious over a person's existence, the lack of historical contextualization, the focus on individual pathology, the limited possibilities of social change, and the dualistic nature of "private" and "public." But rather than simply reject our psychoanalytic background, some of us sought to compensate for its weaknesses by attempting to link it with Marxist theory.[12] This endeavour had the advantage of bringing into the open the realities of socio-economic or structural context and the notion of class. It also challenged the tendency that ascribed virtually all the problems that people experience to defects in personality development and family relationships.

Some of us had been influenced by humanistic approaches such as the ones developed by Rogers and Maslow, which seriously questioned the entire diagnostic categories that had underpinned clinical social work practice until then.[13] They presented a more optimistic and less pathological view of the individual as compared to Freud. But we were concerned with the over-emphasis on human subjectivity and relationship self-absorption, and the lack of conceptualization of the forces of the structural and historical context.[14] The accent was clearly on the "personal troubles" side of the equation. We sought an articulation of the impact of the "social" side in the tenets of the "critical consciousness" movement[15] and in the anti-psychiatry, labelling, and deviance theories and their subsequent views of "personal troubles."[16] Within this perspective, society and its social arrangements were sick, not the individual. This left some of us quite perplexed over the role of the individual in the construction of social reality and of social problems. There was a surge of interest in the critical theory developed by the Frankfurt School.[17] From a Marxist perspective, the latter tries to account for the development of personality problems within an oppressive social system. One of the faculty members assessed the relevance of this perspective for social work practice.[18]

In the search for a theoretical framework that could make sense out of the individual and environmental processes, systems theory seemed to offer the most promise.[19] It shifted the exclusive attention given to the internal psyche to clients or the exclusive focus on the environment, i.e., the family, the school, the neighbourhood, etc. It stressed the dynamic interaction between the individual and the environment and the necessity for some type of balance between the two. While it offered a general unifying framework for social work theory and practice, many of us felt that it neglected to address the relationship between "person-social" in terms of the power of one system over the other, and it failed as well to consider the historical context. The issues of gender, race, class, and ideology were rarely addressed by the advocates of systems theory.[20] In practice, as Carniol and Langan among others point out, systems approaches leave a lot to be desired when it comes to social change.[21]

The contributions of feminism to the development of a progressive curriculum were most significant. Feminism challenged the taken-for-granted assumptions about social work theory, practice, research, and education, and the commitment of feminism to the "personal" and the "political" within a dialectical perspective led to the search for approaches that embraced *both* personal and social change.[22] Since gender cannot be separated from issues of race and class, special attention was given to the conditions of poor and minority women, who are overrepresented among social work clients and who are often overlooked by social work educators and practitioners.

A feminist critique of major theorists who had an impact on social work – Sigmund Freud, Talcott Parsons, and Karl Marx, among others – uncovered widespread inattention to women's needs, misrepresentation of the female experience, routine accept-ance and reinforcement of traditional gender-role stereotypes, and the oppression of women even in the social work profession itself.[23] Feminist research on practitioners' attitudes also unco-vered deep-rooted stereotypes about female and male roles with consequent implications for individual and family interventions, the organization and delivery of social services, and the develop-ment of social welfare policy. Even the experience of learning and teaching was found to contain gender stereotypes that challenged the traditional approaches to curriculum delivery.

The search for an integrative framework to account for the dia-lectical relationships between the "private" and the "public" is still incomplete. There is an uneasiness among many professors in Carleton's School of Social Work with the identification of their endeavour with the "radical" tradition found in Great Britain and the United States.[24] While there are affinities with many of the tenets of this tradition, the concept of "radical" is not a rallying one. Neither is the concept of "Marxist" practice developed by Leonard.[25] While feminism plays a key role in the curriculum, it does not provide the rallying framework. Rather, the present ori-entation of the "collective" is a mix of critical theory (Marxist theories and radical humanism) and feminist theories, which is not without its problems. An attempt was made to link some components of these orientations into a "structural approach," which was originally applied to practice with individuals, groups, families, and communities.[26] In a recent publication, Moreau and Leonard acknowledge that critical (i.e., materialist and Marxist) and feminist theories associated with radical structuralism cur-rently form the underpinnings of the structural approach as they conceive it.[27] This is not also without many ambiguities. Students and practitioners often wonder about the meaning of "structural" and sometimes associate it with traditions of structuralism or structural functionalism, which have little in common with the approach pursued at Carleton.[28] To some extent, the debates that spring from the notion of "structural" are all grist for the mill of critical discourse in a university education. The special attention given to class, gender, and race gives the structural approach a particular originality in social work education.

In a survey of graduates of the School since 1974, Moreau and Leonard attempted to identify more specifically the characteristics of the approach for practitioners and its general relevance for helping people. The majority of respondents noted that while the role of both macro- and micro-level factors were emphasized, the macro or structural factors (i.e., race, gender, class) were seen as overdetermining micro factors. They also perceived a clear emphasis on the analysis of power at all levels, a community approach, and client empowerment as intervention strategies. Moreau and Leonard identify the limitations of this approach, especially around skills development, the role of the individual, the importance of working with internalized forms of oppression, organizational resistance, and the like, and make specific recommendations as to how to change these in a progressive curriculum.[29] Many of these recommendations are already implemented in the present program of the School.

Moreau and Leonard's research has the merit of pointing out that a progressive perspective such as the structural approach is more than a theoretical or analytical exercise. The experience of many graduates of the School relative to the practical relevance of the approach is most promising. Also noteworthy is the fact that the progressive nature of the analysis and practice of the orientation has not escaped the attention or sympathy of many practitioners.

There remain many challenges in the development of a progressive orientation at the School. However, there seems to be a general agreement in the principle that dualistic perspectives are unacceptable and that any serious study of "private troubles" and "public issues" must take into account the *dialectic* between the structural context, i.e., class, gender, ethnicity, and age, on the one hand, and the individual's life, personality structure, and personal resistance, on the other.

Some Curriculum Features

Turning the objectives deriving from a dialectical perspective between "personal troubles" and "private issues" into a Master's curriculum is a formidable challenge. A conscious effort to apply a progressive approach was initially attempted in the core curriculum. The course "Human Behaviour and the Structural Context," which was previously given in two separate courses, one focusing on social processes and the other on psychological processes, was one of the major arenas in which professors and students sought an integrative framework. Significant attention was given to the role of the state, ideology, mediating institutions such as the family and the school, the role of gender, class, and race in shaping human behaviour, and the role of the individual in creating personal and social reality. A critique of contemporary social sciences was made. A major focus of the course was on the position of women in the family, the paid labour force, and the social services. This course still faces the challenge of dealing with fragmented approaches and is a sort of barometer of the ongoing struggle to develop a coherent theoretical framework linking the "personal" and the "social."

Similar experiences occurred in the revision of the "Direct Intervention" course, formerly called "Social Casework." With the participation of faculty, students, practitioners, and visiting professors known for their progressive work, such as Peter Leonard, Carel Germain, and Jeffry Galper,[30] a general framework for practice was developed, chiefly through the efforts of Maurice Moreau. The originality of the approach was the systematic attention given to work, class, gender, and race in the assessment of problems experienced by individuals, families, groups, and communities. Strategies for intervention stressed the roles of brokerage, mediation, and advocacy, with less emphasis on the roles of therapist. Borrowing heavily from Paulo Freire and the feminist movement, these strategies emphasized dialogical relationships with clients and to consciousness-raising practices,[31] and a critique of gender and racial stereotypes in assessment and intervention was developed.

Similar efforts at revising the curriculum occurred in the development of the core courses "History and Philosophy of Social Welfare," "Social Policy Administration," and "Evaluation of Social Work Practice and Social Programs." There were systematic attempts at considering the structural context of practice, policy, and research.

While gender, class, and race variables were considered in the structural course, they were not given the same weight in the other core courses. The emphasis was mostly on class, material conditions, and conflict analyses. The School offered only an elective course on "Women and Welfare." The discussions and debates surrounding the decision to introduce a compulsory course based on a gender analysis were most revealing of the "patriarchal" nature of education and indicated as well an on-going ambivalence about "forcing" anyone, particularly men, to take a course based on women's perspectives on the assessment of problems and their resolutions. At present, the students have the option of taking either the "Human Behaviour and Structural Context" or the "Women and Welfare" course. There is a conscious effort to consider gender along with class and ethnicity in all the courses of the School. To my knowledge, Carleton was the first school in Canada where the systematic inclusion of structural variables was attempted in all the core courses. Even in the "Evaluation of Social Work Practice" course an attempt is made to account for the relevance of feminist research methodologies and the ways in which sexism and racism have penetrated the entire research process, including the formulation of the research questions, the definition of concepts, the construction of variables, the selection of samples, and the interpretation of findings.

Students are introduced to a core content that stresses a dialectical relationship between personal and structural variables, yet they are exposed to a wide range of different viewpoints in these core courses, as well as in the many electives offered in the curriculum.

Curriculum Delivery Issues

While the development of a progressive curriculum had theoretical and practical implications, it also had significant repercussions on the management of the School, the learning/teaching transactions both in the classroom and in the field, and the relationship with the community at large.

Management Issues

At the onset, students had been actively involved in curriculum changes but had not played a significant role in the decision-making structures of the School. In a spirit they considered congruent with the orientation of the School, the students pressed for parity on the School's Board and on all committees related to it. This participatory and democratic approach, which was agreed upon by the majority of the faculty members, while congruent with the School's orientation, was not as congruent with the university's administrative style. There was initially a period of scepticism expressed by some senior administrators as to who was running the School. Over the years, however, student parity did not prove to be an obstacle to program development and decision-making in the School of Social Work. On the contrary, it proved to be an invaluable input into monitoring the quality of the curriculum.

An interesting and perhaps unanticipated consequence of student-faculty parity is the impact this had on the style of management of the School. Scientific/rational management approaches would hardly fit this orientation. Human relations management approaches, with their emphasis on mutual trust and power-sharing, seemed more appropriate but did not account for diverse and often conflicting interests in the School and the inevitability of conflict among students and faculty and among each other. Some questions were even raised about "the ways in which we treat our secretaries like slaves." This led to an examination of the way the academic staff and students made demands of our secretarial support and ancillary staff. The School became a reflection of the forces at play in any social service organization and students had the opportunity to learn how to apply what they had learned in the classroom. And in grading students, professors and the Director had to deal with the inevitable tension of being providers of services and authority figures.

Learning-Teaching Issues

Tension was also present in the teaching-learning process. The traditional and dominant pedagogical style of most classrooms, which emphasizes lecturing and rewards competition, was and still is challenged by many students. The orientation of the School lent itself to dialogical relationships and progressive education. The ways in which the classroom reinforced gender and racial stereotypes were especially targeted, and approaches were suggested to correct this following intensive study sessions attended by both faculty and students. Team teaching became a practice in core courses but because of the size of many of the classes, individualization of learning is still problematic. More flexibility and creativity in course assignments and course evaluations occurred (example: group work was encouraged), but professors had to consider the requirements of the university that an individual grade had to be assigned in such a way to allow a student to appeal the decision if (s)he wishes to do so.

Even though the university calendar explicitly describes the School's orientation and the different courses, many students do not select Carleton to become "radical" or "progressive" social workers. A number of these students experience some of the core courses as indoctrination, an opinion shared by some professional social workers in the community. This disturbing indictment was addressed by students, faculty, and field instructors, who pointed out that many other courses were as vulnerable to this accusation, though they escaped the charge through presenting politically "safe" material only. Furthermore, as mentioned before, diverse views are presented in the core courses and students are exposed to different viewpoints in the many electives offered at the School. Indeed, there are pressures each year from many students not only to maintain the orientation of the School but to extend it to *all* courses. We are accused of diluting the progressive outlook by allowing a pluralist approach to education. This is also a feeling shared by some faculty members. Given the present educational context this tension is inevitable.

There is no doubt that ideological dilemmas are raised for students by the course content. This is not surprising considering the increasing number of students who identify themselves as coming from a middle-class background. A feminist critique of the family, for instance, has a "personal" dimension as well as a "social" component. The Feminist Caucus – the first one in a Canadian School of Social Work – and many other support groups in the School have facilitated the process of consciousness-raising involved in confronting issues raised in the curriculum. More attention, however, has to be given to this process on an ongoing basis.

A remarkable amount of activism by students and professors was always present in the School. Faculty members are not only active in different associations and boards but they have been involved in pressure groups to promote Native rights and better day-care policies, housing policies, facilities and services for battered women and children, etc. Many are active in the labour movement and have been seen on picket lines to support the Children's Aid Society workers and other workers on strike. The Students' Union took a strong stance against pornography on the university campus and is quite active in the social issues concerning women and minority groups. Students have also sought to effect change within the School's curriculum and its delivery. The Race Advisory Committee, for instance, has organized several panels of experts to inform the School community on how to add content on racism and Native issues. Students organized a site visit at the Kingston Penitentiary for Women, where a group of Native women gave an all-day seminar on their experiences as recipients of social work services. A large number of professors and students attended this event. These consciousness-raising experiences were significant in the ongoing revision of the School's policies regarding recruitment of visible minorities and the inclusion of relevant content on race in the curriculum.

A survey of publications of professors and of theses and research essays of students done for the Canadian Association of Schools of Social Work accreditation study and the appraisal of the Ontario Council of Graduate Studies indicate a great deal of preoccupation with social change, a critical analysis of personal and social problems, and a search for alternative approaches for the resolution of these problems.

Fieldwork Issues

In the spirit of the orientation of the School, students took an active role in the selection of their own fieldwork placements by consulting with field instructors and other students to determine the educational value of a given setting. This process has been refined and maintained despite some initial uneasiness in the field and in the faculty. The process of giving students power and choice in where they do their placements led to the development of a learning contract between the student, the field instructor, and the faculty field consultant. Each party agreed to fulfil certain obligations during the period of the field placement. While some field instructors and faculty had some mixed feelings about this arrangement, most of them considered that this change resulted in their students being highly motivated and being able to get involved in the placement much more quickly. But this approach to selection of placements meant that some settings were not used, a fact that has resulted in some criticism; it also raised the issue of making choices among large numbers of students who had selected the same "popular" setting. The co-ordination of field practice became a "diplomatic" as well as a negotiating task.

When the orientation of the practice courses changed, the general view was that the School should offer more placements in progressive and innovative settings. A considerable amount of time and effort was put into reaching and developing these new placements. Examples of these are women's centres and trade unions, which traditionally had not been seen as areas for placing students. Some of these settings had no professional social workers on staff, which raised the issue of supervision of students in these placements. One of the outcomes of the use of alternative settings was that students and some faculty began to think that the School's approach could only be practised in a "progressive" setting, and that all of social work is conservative and all community work radical. This became a major concern for many of us involved in the teaching of practice courses. A conscious effort was made to demonstrate that all methods of social work have the potential to be conservative or progressive.

Indeed, most of our students are doing their placements in so-called "traditional" settings such as hospitals, schools, and family and children agencies.

Skills training was an issue raised by both students and field instructors. Students wanted specific skills to take with them to their placements. They felt that practice courses stressed analytical skills more than the technical skills of interviewing. As a result of pressure from within the School and from the field, skills workshops are now offered in addition to the skills taught in methods courses. There is, however, a constant preoccupation with how to locate skills training within an analytic framework rather than in a vacuum. The transfer of knowledge from the classroom to the field, and from the field to the classroom, still remains an area of much concern in the School and in the field.

Finally, one of the significant challenges facing the School in relation to field practice is the education of field instructors. Some of the course content is unfamiliar to many of those who completed their studies years ago. Furthermore, while many of them are sympathetic to the orientation of the School, they are often uneasy with their lack of knowledge of current trends. Several workshops have been offered to field instructors, but a more systematic attempt must be made to ensure a proper transfer of knowledge from the classroom to the field. Many of our field instructors are former graduates, which facilitates this process.

Reactions of the Community to the School's Orientation

The development of a progressive curriculum in a school originally known for its "clinical" orientation was perceived initially with scepticism and ambivalence. Many alumni and members of professional associations had difficulty identifying with the new orientation, which they saw as anti-clinical, anti-professional, and too preoccupied with "leftist" causes imbued with Marxism and feminism. Some agencies were reluctant to hire graduates, whom they perceived as being too "radical" and not sufficiently identified with the profession's code of ethics. Students themselves expressed concern over these perceptions and were anxious about finding employment.

There remains some friction between the School and the community, but much of it has subsided. The graduates of the School have proven to be competent practitioners with an ability to work in most settings. The participation of faculty members, in various community and professional associations, lent visibility to and demystified the orientation of the School. There is no doubt, however, that a certain tension must exist between practice and education. We should be related as closely as we can to practice, yet should remain separate enough that we can examine, be critical, and make our contribution to practice.

Conclusion

The experience in connecting "private troubles" and "public issues" into a progressive curriculum at Carleton University's School of Social Work has been exciting but troublesome. The development of the program is an ongoing process, and it is still a struggle, full of conflicts, anxieties, and ambiguities. It is not a search for a particular "true" way, and there is by no means any unanimity over its future. A shift in paradigmatic orientation[32] is always problematic, for it involves personal as well as socio-political dimensions. Many of us have learned – often painfully – not to underestimate the impact of both of these dimensions.

Schools of social work, which ultimately must remain dedicated to the people in our society whom practitioners try to serve and work with, are still located within the boundaries of university bureaucracies, professional communities, associations, and state organizations. A shift away from the status quo must take into account the interests of each of these constituencies and develop clear strategies to deal with them. This requires not only a "structural" analysis but the establishment and maintenance of a strong "collective" among school members, including students, which allows for the development of analytical and practice frameworks. In a university environment that stresses individual achievement and competition, this is no easy task. We have recognized the importance of developing coalitions with other professors in the university and in other universities, and with practitioners in the community who were struggling with the same issues. Through organizing conferences, special seminars, visiting professorships, and the like, we have been able to refine our analysis and maintain the courage to carry on.

The analysis of both the personal and the socio-political dimensions is crucial in any attempt at social change. Social structures are also maintained by people's beliefs and ideologies, which do not change simply by rational debates. Many of us were often impatient, if not intolerant, of so-called "personal resistance" to change. We have learned, again often painfully, that one must believe in the "process," a concept often referred to in the feminist literature. There is a danger of falling into dogmatism and labelling if one is not conscious of the personal dimensions involved in any social change. Dealing with colleagues, students, and professional social workers who do not share our point of view and our enthusiasm requires commitment and faith in the process and a constant examination of our own contradictions regarding class, gender, and race. Some of us, for example, joined or formed consciousness-raising groups such as the Feminist Caucus and Men's Group, which dealt specifically with these issues. Anyone committed to social change, it would seem, should be involved in some type of personal "critical consciousness" exercise, as described by Freire.[33]

To confront the inequities in capitalism, in patriarchy, and in racism and to evolve more equitable practice strategies that meet these objectives requires a great deal of courage and humility. These attributes can only come from realizing the complexity of the personal and socio-political dimensions involved in any change. It is a process, an unfinished project that demands a clear commitment both to the process itself and to its continuous outcome.

Notes

1. William Schwartz, "Private Troubles and Public Issues: One Social Work Job or Two?" in Paul E. Weinberger, ed., *Perspectives on Social Welfare*, 2nd edition (New York: Macmillan, 1974), pp. 346-62.
2. See Mary Richmond, "The Retail Method of Reform," in Joanna C.

Colcord and R.Z.S. Mann, eds., *The Long View: Papers and Addresses by Mary Richmond* (New York: Russell Sage Foundation, 1930), pp. 214-21; Porter R. Lee, "Social Work: Cause and Function," in *Proceedings of the National Conference of Social Work 1929* (Chicago: University of Chicago Press, 1930), pp. 3-20; Clarke A. Chambers, "An Historical Perspective on Political Action vs. Individualized Treatment," in *Current Issues in Social Work Seen in Historical Perspective* (New York: Council on Social Work Education, 1962).

3. See, for example, Paul Halmos, *The Personal and the Political: Social Work and Political Action* (London: Hutchinson and Co., 1978), Chapter 6.

4. Schwartz, "Private Troubles and Public Issues."

5. See Helen Levine, "The Personal Is Political: Feminism and the Helping Professions," in Angela Miles and Geraldine Finn, eds., *Feminism in Canada* (Montreal: Black Rose Books, 1982), pp. 175-210; Mary Bricker-Jenkins and Nancy R. Hooyman, eds., *Not For Women Only: Social Work Practice for a Feminist Future* (Silver Spring, Md.: NASW, 1986).

6. David Austin, "The Flexner Myth and the History of Social Work," *Social Service Review*, 57 (September, 1983), pp. 357-77.

7. For this reciprocal, dynamic model, see David Webb, "Themes and Continuities in Radical and Traditional Social Work," *British Journal of Social Work*, 11 (1981), pp. 143-58; Carolyn Morell, "Cause *is* Function: Toward a Feminist Model of Integration for Social Work," *Social Service Review*, 61, 1 (March, 1987), pp. 146-55.

8. Hans S. Falck, *Social Work: The Membership Perspective* (New York: Springer Publishing, 1988), pp. 1-28.

9. See C. Wright Mills, *The Sociological Imagination* (New York: Oxford University Press, 1959), p. 187.

10. David Webb, "Social Work and Critical Consciousness: Rebuilding Orthodoxy," *Issues in Social Work Education*, 5, 2 (Winter, 1985), pp. 89-102; J. Longres and E. MacLeod, "Consciousness Raising and Social Work Practice," *Social Casework*, 61, 5 (1980), p. 272.

11. See Paul H. Ephross and Michael Reisch, "The Ideology of Some Social Work Texts," *Social Service Review* (June, 1982), pp. 273-91.

12. Richard Lichtman, *The Production of Desire: The Integration of Psychoanalysis into Marxist Theory* (New York: The Free Press, 1982); Russell Jacoby, *Social Amnesia: A Critique of Contemporary Psychology from Adler to Laing* (Boston: Beacon Press, 1975).

13. C.R. Rogers, *Client-Centered Therapy* (Boston: Houghton-Mifflin, 1951); A. Maslow, *Towards a Psychology of Being* (New York: Van Nostrand, 1968).

14. See E.M. Schur, *The Awareness Trap* (New York: Quadrangle, 1976).
15. Bernard Davies, "Towards a Personalist Framework for Radical Social Work Education," in Roy Bailey and Phil Lee, eds., *Theory and Practice in Social Work* (Oxford: Basil Blackwell, 1982), pp. 171–87; Thomas Keefe, "Empathy Skill and Critical Consciousness," *Social Casework*, 61, 7 (September, 1980), pp. 387–93; Paulo Freire, *Education for Critical Consciousness* (New York: Seabury Press, 1973).
16. Geoffrey Pearson, *The Deviant Imagination: Psychiatry, Social Work and Social Change* (London: Macmillan, 1975); Halmos, *The Personal and the Political*; Jacoby, *Social Amnesia*.
17. For elaboration of the critical theory, see Martin Jay, *The Dialectical Imagination* (Toronto: Little, Brown and Co., 1973).
18. Peter Findlay, "Critical Theory and Social Work Practice," *Catalyst*, No. 3 (1978), pp. 53–68.
19. Full discussions of systems theory are to be found in Ludwig von Bertalanffy, *General Systems Theory* (New York: George Braziller, 1968); Walter Buckley, *Sociology and Modern Systems Theory* (Englewood Cliffs, N.J.: Prentice-Hall, 1967).
20. See Helen Marchant, "Gender, Systems Thinking and Radical Social Work," in Helen Marchant and Betsy Wearing, eds., *Gender Reclaimed: Women in Social Work* (Sydney: Southwood Press, 1986), pp. 14–32.
21. See Ben Carniol, "Clash of Ideologies in Social Work Education," *Canadian Social Work Review* (1984), pp. 184–200; M. Langan, "The Unitary Approach: A Feminist Critique," in Eve Brooks and Ann Davis, eds., *Women, the Family, and Social Work* (London: Tavistock, 1985), pp. 28–47. See also Chapter 1 of this book.
22. Levine, "The Personal Is Political"; Morell, "Cause is Function."
23. See, for example, Michele Barrett, *Women's Oppression Today: Problems in Marxist Feminist Analysis* (Thetford, Norfolk: The Thetford Press, 1985); Red Collective, *The Politics of Sexuality in Capitalism* (London: Red Collective and Publications Distribution Co-op, 1978).
24. For Great Britain, see Webb, "Themes and Continuities in Radical and Traditional Social Work"; for the U.S., see Jeffry Galper, *Social Work Practice: A Radical Perspective* (Englewood Cliffs, N.J.: Prentice-Hall, 1980).
25. Peter Leonard, "Towards a Paradigm for Radical Practice," in Roy Bailey and Mike Brake, eds., *Radical Social Work* (London: Edward Arnold, 1975), pp. 46–61.
26. See Maurice Moreau, "A Structural Approach to Social Work Practice," *Canadian Journal of Social Work Education*, 5, 1 (1979), pp. 78–94.

27. Maurice Moreau and Lynne Leonard, *Empowerment Through a Structural Approach to Social Work. A Report From Practice* (Ottawa: Carleton University, 1989).

28. For structuralism, see David Robey, ed., *Structuralism* (Oxford: Clarendon Press, 1976); Richard and Fernando De George, *The Structuralists from Marx to Levi-Strauss* (Garden City, N.Y.: Doubleday, 1972). For structural functionalism, see Talcott Parsons, *The Social System* (New York: The Free Press, 1951); Robert Merton, "Manifest and Latent Functions," in *On Theoretical Sociology* (New York: The Free Press, 1968), pp. 73–138.

29. Moreau and Leonard, *Empowerment*.

30. See Leonard, "Towards a Paradigm for Radical Practice"; Carel B. Germain, ed., *Social Work Practice: People and Environments: An Ecological Perspective* (New York: Columbia University Press, 1980); Jeffry Galper, *The Politics of Social Services* (Englewood Cliffs, N.J.: Prentice-Hall, 1975).

31. See Moreau, "A Structural Approach."

32. See Thomas Kuhn, *The Structure of Scientific Revolutions* (Cambridge: Cambridge University Press, 1962).

33. Freire, *Education for Critical Consciousness*.

CHAPTER 3

Social Work and the Women's Movement

by Joan Gilroy

Introduction

The women's movement and feminism have been significant influences for a number of students, faculty, and practitioners in reconceptualizing social work and in developing what has been called feminist practice, that is, social work practice rooted in an awareness of women's inequality and based on an analysis of how systemic injustice shapes personal and social life. Feminist practice helps women to make sense of personal problems in the wider context of exploitation and oppression and, consequently, is directed toward empowerment.

The re-emergence of the women's movement in the last twenty or so years has resulted in broad public awareness of women's inequality, ground-breaking scholarship about women and gender, and new organizations and services to improve the position of women. Transition houses for battered women, rape crisis centres, feminist counselling, and health services were all established under the auspices of the women's movement. The experience of organizing to bring about broad social change and alternative services for women stimulated feminists in social work to try to use what we had learned from the women's movement in our own practice and in schools of social work.

As we began the process of combining feminism and social work, we were very hopeful about the possibilities for transforming social work to make it more humane, more oriented toward the lives of women, and more effective in contributing to the broader changes needed for women's equality. Once we began to apply our rapidly increasing knowledge about women's oppression, however, we began to encounter enormous obstacles to doing social work in ways that are compatible with feminist awareness. We discovered that social workers, women and men alike, often feel threatened by feminism and the broader women's movement. In the view of many of our students and colleagues, feminist analysis of major social problems, feminist critiques of professional practice, and feminist ways of fostering personal and social change are marginal rather than central to the practice of social work.

The purpose of this chapter is to explore both the difficulties and the possibilities for developing feminist practice in social work. First, however, we need to consider three basic questions: What is the women's movement? What is feminism? And, why is it difficult to use what has been learned from them in social work?

The Women's Movement and Feminism

The women's movement and feminism are complex, interacting, and changing and, therefore, difficult to define. The women's movement is the more general term, and it identifies a social movement that encompasses many diverse activities that have been directed at furthering women's broad struggle for equality and justice.[1] Throughout its long history, the women's movement has taken different forms according to the social and political circumstances in which it has arisen.[2] During the movement's earlier stages in Western countries, women emphasized the attainment of legal and political rights – the right to education, to own certain property, to vote, and to hold political office.[3] Few will forget that Canadian women became "persons" under the law in 1929 thanks to the work of Emily Murphy, Nellie McClung, and other women.

The so-called second wave of the women's movement emerged in the late 1960s and 1970s and has been an important impetus for social and political change throughout the world. Rather than focus on rights, women have taken a broader view of what is necessary for liberation. Virtually every facet of social life has been analysed from the perspectives of women. Enormous efforts have been made to end the poverty, violence, and despair in which so many women live, and to prevent the discrimination that occurs as a routine feature of women's lives. The goals of the current movement can be summarized as economic, legal, and political equality; reproductive control; and the right to choose in areas such as employment and sexual orientation. The women's movement has also explored the material and ideological changes needed to make choices meaningful. For example, campaigns waged for pay equity, child care, and equal opportunities in education and against sexual harassment have all affected women's choices in relation to employment.

Fundamental themes and beliefs permeate feminism and the women's movement. The most basic are a consciousness of the inequality of women, a sense of injustice about this, and a commitment to overcome exploitation based on sex/gender. "The personal is political," a famous slogan of the women's movement, captures another unifying theme. Women began to see that problems such as physical abuse, which had been considered individual and unique, were in fact common and widespread, and were rooted in women's social and political subordination. "Political" is used here in the sense of having to do with power. Men's violence toward women has been directly connected with men having a disproportionate share of wealth and power. Claiming the right to talk with each other about experiences such as violence, the authority to try to understand and explain their own lives, and the power to change themselves and society are also central to the women's movement.

While overall objectives are shared, there is considerable diversity within the women's movement. In fact, there is no one women's movement, no one leader or group of leaders, no one organization, and no one method of bringing about women's liberation. Rather, there are many movements, many issues and organizations, and many ways of participating. Women vary widely in terms of social class, race, sexual orientation, marital status, age, abilities and disabilities. They therefore have different experiences of inequality and different ways of understanding and fighting against subordination and oppression.

The impact of the women's movement on our consciousness and our behaviour is undeniable. The work of countless women has achieved positive changes in law and social policy and in everyday life. Yet, serious inequities and problems persist. Women continue to earn less than men even when their qualifications, experience, and type of work are the same or comparable.[4] Men's violence against women continues and may be increasing. Feminism explains why this is so and helps one understand women's oppression, how it works in concrete ways in the world and in our own lives, and how it can be changed.

Like the women's movement, feminism encompasses many meanings.[5] The best definitions capture the notions of analysis and process. Nancy Hartsock, for example, says feminism is "a mode of analysis, a method of approaching life and politics, a way of asking questions and searching for answers, rather than a set of political conclusions about the oppression of women."[6] Helen Levine speaks of feminism as a framework for understanding the situation of women and for guiding the process of counselling.[7] Feminism offers no single theory of women's oppression, for no such theory exists or is likely to be found. Similarly, feminism does not and ought not prescribe one way to live or one correct set of beliefs and values.

The diversity within feminism has been most often discussed in relation to the traditional spectrum of philosophical and political ideas. Hence, the terms "liberal feminism," "Marxist feminism," "socialist feminism," and "radical feminism" are used to describe varying explanations of and solutions to the problem of women's oppression.[8] Feminists are also named according to their sexual orientation and race.[9] Whatever the differences are called, they have been influential in shaping our understanding of the basis of oppression, the nature and extent of the changes believed necessary, and the most effective strategies for achieving equality for women.

At this point, I want to say something about my own understanding of feminism and the women's movement. We all write and speak and act on the basis of particular experiences, which are shaped by our location in the social world and which influence our analysis and strategies.[10] Women's inequality is deeply embedded in the world in which we live, particularly in the systemic differences in wealth and power between women and men, among different races, and between the developed and developing countries. Hence, women's oppression can only be eliminated as part of the process of all people acquiring a fair share of the world's goods and the power necessary to determine how these resources will be used. In other words, human societies must be changed in fundamental ways to eliminate systemic inequalities of all types. For me, feminism also means acting in solidarity with women to improve social conditions and acting in ways that empower women. In addition, feminism offers ways of linking women's inequality with that of other peoples, with blacks and aboriginal people, with the old, the sick, and the disabled, to name only some disadvantaged groups, and of supporting other liberation movements.

In trying to use what has been learned from the women's movement, feminists in social work have encountered difficulties and barriers. The following section will explore some characteristics that make social work problematic ground for building feminist practice.

Social Work – Traditional and Radical Perspectives

Social work, like the women's movement and feminism, is not a single entity. Forms of practice and theories vary and change over time. Significant differences in overall orientation to the profession and to the social services are frequently represented by broad categories such as traditional and radical social work. Keeping in mind that all categorizations oversimplify and distort reality and do not necessarily correspond with the actual experiences of individuals, we will use these categories, *traditional* and *radical*, to identify some of the essential differences in approaches.

Traditional definitions of social work emphasize the themes of helping persons in their social environments, the interdependence of individuals and society, and personal and social change.[11] Humanitarian values, the ability to establish professional helping relationships, the use of theory about human behaviour, and systematic problem-solving techniques have all been stressed in social work.

Conventional social work often includes the assumption that individuals are more powerful than social conditions in creating problems. In this respect, it reflects the dominant belief system, the dominant ideology, of the larger society. Human beings are seen as unique, as members of a particular family, as self-determining, and as experiencing private troubles requiring confidential professional treatment. Factors such as gender, race, social class, and age are not explicitly viewed as systemic determinants of opportunities for jobs, education, health, and material resources. People are assumed to interact with one another and with social institutions on an individual, free, and relatively equal basis. Social welfare policy and programs, developed by neutral (if not benevolent) governments, are understood to express wide agreement on values and human needs. As a consequence of these beliefs, the foundation of professional social work is considered to be the knowledge and skills required to work with individuals and families on what are seen as personal problems.

Criticisms from the political left have particularly influenced feminist social workers. Radical, Marxist, socialist, and structural approaches all rest on a fundamental critique of social work and social welfare institutions in capitalist societies. Capitalism is an economic and social form that favours the owners of capital, the rich and powerful, at the expense of those who sell their labour, the ill, the old, and all who are disadvantaged in relation to producing for profit. From a radical perspective, the ways of accumulating and distributing wealth and power change in accordance with historical circumstances, but the inherent systemic injustices of capitalism remain. Further, the structures for producing wealth impose relations of hierarchy, of domination and subordination between people and among groups of people. The boss/worker or master/servant relationship is a prototype of social relations under capitalism. In short, these critics see capitalism as the root of personal and social problems and as shaping social institutions such as the state in the interests of the powerful few rather than according to the needs of all people.[12]

Social services are shown to be enmeshed in and to reflect the inherent inequalities and contradictions of capitalism. While radicals appreciate that welfare policy and services provide some real benefits, they do not see the dominant effect as progressive but as shoring up an unfair system by helping the casualties of capitalism. Further, a radical perspective views the current social programs as having been established and as being administered as though people's poverty and other problems were caused by themselves or were accidental, rather than being the result of systematic injustice. Social workers employed in the current system recognize many barriers and frustrations in doing the work of helping. They are concerned about the people with whom they work and about the quality of the service they can provide. Clearly, most social workers realize that social programs are inadequate to meet clients' needs, but they do not often connect these limitations to larger social forces. Neither their socialization as people nor their education for social work include, in most cases, an analysis of how economic and political systems work to the disadvantage of most service users. According to a radical analysis, then, social workers do not challenge the unfairness of the welfare system because they lack awareness of the systemic nature of social problems flowing from inequalities in wealth and power.

In addition, social workers are not in a good position to criticize because most are employed by government agencies, which administer mandated welfare services. In contrast to the predominant view of governments as impartial, radical scholars show them to be aligned with the interests of the powerful and to act rather consistently to support those interests.[13] The state can be seen as an institution or a group of institutions and as a form of social relations.[14] Institutions commonly understood to be included are the legislature, the courts, the military, education, health, and social services. Certain financial powers also belong to the state. The bureaucratic form of organization found in government agencies, including social agencies, depends on a hierarchy of authority, control, and salary. Such an arrangement creates relationships of inequality among people – for example, between social workers and their clients and between social workers and their supervisors and administrators.

Social workers and clients alike know something is wrong with the services provided, and they experience obstacles in working closely and co-operatively, but they do not normally see the problems as created by state policies and agencies. These arguments, which are only sketched here, are part of a wider debate about the relationship between the state and social welfare programs and as such contributed to feminist understanding of these programs and professional practice.

Feminist Critiques

Feminists raise fundamental questions about the ways social science has explained women, men, and social life.[15] The most frequent criticism in all disciplines is that women either have been left out of social and political theory or their experiences have been misrepresented along sexist lines. Feminist scholars argue, for example, that neither conventional social science nor traditional Marxism or socialism have understood women's position in the family and in the labour force, and that they have not adequately accounted for the economic and social value of women's domestic and paid work. As a consequence of this lack of understanding of women's position, social policy reflects conservative notions of women and men in the family and in the economy. Social policy is developed by governments, that is, by elected politicians and by top-ranking civil servants. This political process, however, is dominated by male politicians, who are usually also wealthy, white, and socially connected to one another and to powerful interest groups in the broader society.[16] Most chief civil servants are men, too.

Since women and gender have not been topics for conventional research and women have been excluded from political processes, it is not surprising that social welfare policy and services are not informed by an analysis of women's inequality and exploitation in the private sphere of home and family and in public spheres such as employment. As Elizabeth Wilson points out, governments define women primarily in terms of their relationships to men and their work (usually called "role") as wives and mothers in the family and home.[17] To be sure, men continue to be seen in terms of their employment and their financial responsibilities for wives or women partners and children. (Witness the struggle in Nova Scotia to extend family benefits through the provincial welfare program to single-parent fathers.) Although men's roles often limit their human potential and their jobs can be degrading and dehumanizing, their work is more highly valued both economically and socially.

It is not just a question of social attitudes about what is right and proper for women and men to do. Rather, it is a failure to recognize that women's labour is essential to both the bearing and raising of children and to the creation of material goods, that is, to both reproduction and production. The sexual division of labour and its effects are well documented. Women are not seen as workers at home and are not paid equally with men in the labour market. Women are poor, especially those who are lone parents.[18] In fact, poverty among women is so widespread that we now talk about the feminization of poverty. If women's domestic labour were assigned its real value, and if there were effective equal pay laws, then there would be much less poverty and less need for social assistance. Most poor families are headed by women. Many of these survive on welfare payments because they cannot support themselves and their children on women's wages.

Social assistance legislation and programs clearly illustrate conservative and stereotypical images of women and men. As shown in a recent study in Nova Scotia, the state enters the lives of single mothers on welfare in very personal, controlling, and sexist ways.[19] These women are expected to raise their children on amounts of money below the recognized minimum costs for food, clothing, and shelter, and this means that they live far below the poverty line.[20] If these women are not able to feed, clothe, house, and care for their children to the satisfaction of child welfare agencies, they may become part of a protection caseload or their children may be taken from them. Women on welfare are afraid they will be found to be unfit mothers and feel threatened by contacts with child welfare workers or, indeed, with most officials from state agencies.

In addition, the regulations surrounding cohabitation, the infamous "man in the house" rule, of several provincial welfare programs are extremely sexist. Under these regulations, women who are suspected of sleeping or living with a man may be cut off welfare benefits immediately without what would normally be regarded as proof or the right to due process. To have her benefits restored, a woman must prove her "innocence." The presumption is that if a woman and man are sleeping or living together, then she is or ought to be getting financial support from him. As a direct result of state social policy, then, women are controlled by the fear of losing their children and of having their personal friendships investigated and by the constant pressure to survive without the material means to do so.

Feminists also argue that major theories in counselling and in social work practice are based on assumptions and explanations that overtly discriminate against women[21] and other subordinate groups such as homosexuals, racial minorities, the poor, and those who are disabled. As noted above, the view expressed here is that the oppression of whole groups of people based on criteria such as gender, sexual orientation, race, and class is linked in complex ways that are not yet fully understood. Although the main focus here is on sexism, it is well to remember that the clients of social services are mainly poor women, many of whom are disabled or members of racial and ethnic minorities.

Family life, mothering or the institution of motherhood, as Adrienne Rich says, and romantic/sexual relations have all been revealed as problematic for women. This is not to say – as feminists are often accused of saying – that there is nothing positive for women about family life. Fortunately, many women experience family life as satisfying and rewarding. Indeed, as Rich has also pointed out, having and caring for children and raising them can be the source of exquisite joy as well as pain.[22]

Family therapy can be taken as one illustration of an area of critical inquiry from the perspectives of women and feminism.[23] Feminist analysis has contributed enormously to our understanding of the family as a site of violence and oppression for women and children as well as the "haven in a heartless world" portrayed in both popular and professional literature. Feminists have said not only that there are problems in the family – this was hardly new – but that these problems occur frequently and are neither accidental nor generally pathological. Instead, problems that appear as personal are intricately connected with the structures of female and male relations to reproduction and production and with inequality between the sexes in the wider society.

Physical violence toward women provides a concrete illustration of sexism in family theory and practice. Women have been battered by their husbands or male partners in their own homes throughout history, but this was viewed as natural and was condoned if not actually encouraged by law and social policy until the women's movement took up this issue.[24] Professional therapists of all types tended to blame the woman for the violence or to see it as the result of interactions between two equal people. Feminists demonstrated that the economic and political inequality between the sexes was manifest in the vast majority of female-male relationships, including marriage or intimate partnerships. Furthermore, women who wanted to leave abusive relationships shared the obstacles they faced. Where would they go? Where would they and their children be safe? Would they be protected by the law and police? Who would help them? Under the auspices of the women's movement, transition houses were established for battered women and their children, and laws and social policies were changed to make it more possible for women to escape violence.

Feminists have developed alternative approaches to counselling and service provision that incorporate principles, processes, and theories learned from working as activists and as scholars.[25] Listening to and believing women who told of rape or battering or incest, sharing experiences more equally, and understanding personal problems in the wider context of oppression have been part of feminist counselling and services. In addition, feminists have tried to establish non-hierarchical or less hierarchical organizations to work co-operatively to support and empower women.

Our discussion thus far has centred on feminism, the women's movement, and social work, which share the goals of personal and social change, which value people and caring relations, and which work toward a more humane world. All involve women helping women, but they use different analyses and methods. Social work practice typically means women employed by government or quasi-government agencies to help other women who are suffering the effects of poverty, bad housing, and generally inadequate resources to do the work of raising their children. Though there are differing orientations in social work, the most prevalent forms of practice make it difficult to use feminist approaches. An illustration of both the obstacles and the possibilities is useful.

I was the faculty field instructor for a very capable mature woman student who was doing her practicum in a child welfare agency. She had had some training and several years of experience in the field before beginning her degree in social work. Although she was beginning to explore women's issues, she was by no means a radical, feminist or otherwise. Early in her placement, she was assigned the following situation.

A woman came to the agency asking that her three children be taken into care temporarily. Her former husband had returned the children without advance notice, thus breaking their agreement that he would look after the children for a specified period while she was getting her life together. She was living in one room, had a low-paying job, and had neither the space nor the money to provide for her children.

When the student social worker discussed this woman's request for temporary care with the agency supervisor, a humane and progressive man, she was asked to appraise the client's "real motivation" to look after her children. The supervisor felt that if the woman client really wanted her children, really wanted to be a mother, she would find suitable housing and child care – this in a city where housing for low-income people was very scarce and where there was at that time a broadly based community social action group formed specifically to campaign for decent affordable housing for poor people.

Later, when the oldest child had to be taken into temporary care because there simply was not enough room for everyone in the mother's one room (the oldest was believed by her mother to be best able to understand why she had to go to a foster home), the student was advised not to record housing as the reason for taking the child into care. This agency, it was explained, did not take children into care primarily because of housing and was not a housing agency. The woman's depression, her disorganization in crisis, and the stress she was under were suggested as the real reasons for temporary foster placement.

Several meetings followed among the student, the agency supervisor, and myself to discuss the issue of motivation and how the reasons for temporary care would be recorded. The student and I argued that motivation could not be fairly assessed out of the context of resources and ought not to be raised with this woman. She said she wanted her children but that she could not continue to keep them in one room, that her income was not sufficient to feed four people, and that her hours of work, over which she had no control, meant that child care was necessary. The student social worker and I believed her, believed that she wanted her children but was not in a position to provide for them. Our approach was to accept her definition of the problem and to see what could be done to muster the resources necessary for the job of mothering. And we did not want to record the reasons for temporary care as the woman's problems – her anxiety about how she was going to look after her children as depression, her coming for help as lack of motivation, and the lack of resources as her disorganization. This woman was very strong and coping well with an extremely difficult situation. Calling her sick or inadequate was untrue and unjust.

Fortunately, the supervisor accepted this approach. The student worked hard to mobilize concrete resources, to find child care and housing, and to provide ongoing support to the client in coping with these very difficult circumstances. Thanks to the client's strength and the student's persistence, they were able to overcome all sorts of obstacles, and the situation had a positive outcome. In fact, almost two years later, the student, now a graduate, recently encountered this particular woman, who said that she and her children were doing well both emotionally and financially.

I wish I could say that this case is an isolated example of a lack of awareness of how the economic and social position of women affects their ability to care for their children and to be healthy and productive themselves. Unfortunately, this situation is not unique but typical. Most of the cases assigned to students in this agency involved single-parent women trying to bring up their children without adequate resources. Yet, the focus of case discussions in staff meetings and in supervisory sessions was often on the individual characteristics of the clients – their motivation or lack of motivation, their dependency, their inability to budget resulting in chronic financial problems and crises, their parenting skills.

It is difficult to account for the persistence of the notion that women, if sufficiently motivated and perhaps especially if they truly want to be mothers, can manage on welfare or, alternatively, can find decent housing, a job that pays enough to support themselves and their children, and affordable day care.[26] The most superficial knowledge of housing, child care, and employment opportunities and incomes for the majority of women, and certainly most single-parent women, does not lend credence to the belief that one person can surmount such obstacles. To act as if the problems of our clients, the majority of whom are women, are primarily individual and can be overcome by their own initiative serves only to undermine clients' abilities and efforts and to erode what little self-esteem they may have salvaged from their lives.

Feminism and the women's movement are powerful forces for change in the world today and have created a broad revolution in consciousness, rich theoretical insights about women's oppression, and alternative women's services. What can be learned from feminism and the women's movement that would enable us to understand the situations of women differently and help more effectively?

Lessons from Feminism and the Women's Movement

Feminists in social work have already begun to create new forms of practice. Feminist social work suggests the necessity of rebuilding theory and practice to account for the oppression and the survival of women and other exploited groups, and to do this in a collective process that empowers women to bring about the radical changes in economic and political structures that will make genuine equality possible.

Rebuilding Social Work Theory/Practice

The first requirement is a redefinition and reconstruction of social work theory and practice built on a profound change in our ways of understanding ourselves and the society in which we live. In short, the values, methods, and goals of social work must be transformed.

Such new theory and practice would necessarily be rooted in an investigation of systemic inequalities in wealth and power. We need to know how these inequalities influence human beings and shape social problems in everyday life. In this building of theory and practice, feminist analysis of inequality and oppression would be a cornerstone and would be incorporated in social work curricula, in continuing education, and in the daily activities of teaching, learning, and doing social work. It is not merely a matter of adding women's issues to what exists in social work education and practice – this is already being done in varying degrees – but of using feminism as a dynamic to transform social work.

In talking about the creation of a new social work, I do not want to leave the impression that feminist theory/practice is out there in the world, like an object, waiting to be discovered and applied to social work. Rather, I think of *building new theory and practice as a process of inquiry, a feminist process* that begins with women, with the ways women describe and make sense of their experiences, and discovers how this compares with what is written in texts and in social policies and with what is done by social workers.

Beginning with those who come as clients is a familiar concept to social workers. Social work has as one of its most basic principles the premise of beginning with the client and moving *with* the client through the process of understanding the needs or problems and working co-operatively toward a solution. Although beginning with the client seems sensible, it is difficult to put into practice. Social workers are often face to face with people whose basic needs are not met, but the social workers themselves do not have the resources or the power to access what is needed to help clients in crises. To make the principle even more difficult to apply, most social workers do their work in a milieu where both problems and solutions are conceptualized predominantly in individual or family and psychological terms.

Social workers can offer counselling and support, can help clients negotiate the maze of services more effectively, and can advocate on their behalf. (It should be noted, however, that advocacy is a skill most social workers have not developed sufficiently, partly because of the belief in the power of the individual, partly because social workers are taught to guard against clients becoming too dependent. Dependency is viewed as a psychological trait and not typically related to oppression or to a lack of resources.) In the end, though, both clients and social workers often know that what clients really need are more resources to do the jobs of living and parenting.

If a social worker is aware of the broad structural forces that shape human lives, she or he is left in the contradictory position of knowing that concrete material resources are needed, that the service offered is not sufficient, and that the conditions under which it is given are dehumanizing and degrading. Helping clients to understand that their problems are not of their own making but are part of larger social and economic forces is a positive way of handling this difficult situation. One feminist social worker put it this way:

I use questions a lot, ask clients what happened, how they explain this, how they feel about it, and what action, if any, they want to take. I say what I think too – I don't lecture about patriarchy or anything like that. I try to listen really carefully to what they're saying, and share my own thinking about their actual situation. I try to support them too, to let them know that I don't think it's their fault, and that I want to help them figure out something to do to help. I use my feminism all the time, but I'm not heavy about it with clients. I try to stay close to their situation, to use my feminism to help the work along.[27]

Developing a feminist consciousness, that is, becoming aware of the inequality and exploitation of women, can be painful, which is perhaps one reason why many social workers resist feminist and structural analyses. As one woman said:

Becoming a feminist has made work very painful for me. I understand so much more, but I find this overwhelming and paralyzing. I may even have been a better social worker before – then, I believed that what we were doing was good and I thought that so much was possible if I worked hard enough. Now, I know that most of my clients will not get off welfare and will remain depressed and overcome by their lives. It's hard to keep doing what you can, to keep yourself up for work.

And, from another feminist colleague:

I seem just to have succeeded in making everyone mad at me. The people at work think I am crazy, that I react too strongly to everything, that I have no patience with the system, that I am too radical and won't be able to get another job when I burn out in this one – they accept burnout as inevitable . . . and, I don't know how much longer I can work here, or where I would find another job . . . or, whether I want to work in social work anymore.

The risks of burnout and of becoming an unemployed feminist are real. Social workers are largely employed by government agencies and government-funded services, which makes the task of analysis particularly difficult. Even in places like transition houses for battered women, criticisms of government policy are considerably weakened if not silenced altogether because most transition houses obtain a major share of their funding from governments.[28]

If social work is to become more involved in the larger goal of women's equality, then social workers must develop a critical consciousness in relation to women's inferior status as a foundation for constructing new theories and strategies. Once this process has begun, however, the enormity of the gap between social work ideals and the actual practice of the profession, between accepted theory and new perspectives, is overwhelming. In the women's movement, collective work enables and enriches the process of creating new theory and new forms of practice and, at the same time, offers the possibility of support to individuals in the process of change.

Working Collectively Toward Empowerment

If we need new theories and new ways of practising that truly account for women and gender, and if this new theory/practice can only be the result of a process, as I have argued, and if this process is difficult and painful, then how can we begin such a process? How can we as social workers overcome the barriers to developing feminist consciousness? How does working collectively help to bring about personal and social changes?

By collective is meant co-operative work among people who develop a shared vision of a world of humanity and justice for all, the goal of remaking social institutions to respond to human needs and to foster equality, and the task of creating ourselves as new people, loving, nurturing, peaceful, and capable of living in community with each other. Collective work, then, is rooted in shared experience and consciousness. Feminist consciousness is born from the experience of being female in a patriarchal society, of living as a woman in a world that treats women as inferior, as incapable of making adult decisions, and as objects of all types of abuse. Women live in very different conditions, but most have experienced sexism in some form. Awareness of the personal effects of oppression is the basis for consciousness and collective work. *Empowerment* is the explicit purpose of collective work. Through working together with some degree of shared experience and consciousness, people empower themselves to change their lives and the world.

Social workers aspiring to work collectively toward empowerment will need to overcome immense barriers. In common with other professions, social work stresses uniqueness rather than commonality, is primarily organized to serve individuals rather than groups, and defines problems as personal more than social and political. Clients are usually interviewed one by one by a social worker, who is supervised by another, who, in turn, is accountable to an administrator. Such a hierarchy means that women workers normally have the responsibility for direct work with clients but little authority over agency policy, budgets, and other resources. Working with clients individually or in family units, however, means that social workers have direct access to how clients experience problems, how they explain and try to deal with them in their daily lives. From a feminist perspective, then, there is the possibility of exploring with clients the connections between personal troubles and systemic inequalities, of connecting people with similar experiences, and of networking with colleagues with common concerns.

Working collectively is clearly promising, though the methods of collective work need to be examined closely for their usefulness to women in the real conditions of social work practice – for instance, the high caseloads and the crisis nature of much of direct practice. The strategies for collective work implied by earlier versions of radical theory and practice did not come out of a grounding in the daily social work practice. In fact, these strategies reflected a male revolutionary model – men as workers made the revolution, organizing in their places of work around issues related to their jobs, and unencumbered by having to make meals or to look after children.

Much can be learned from feminist organizing that may be useful in social work. Feminists have continuously pointed out that women's domestic responsibilities conflict with public life and social change activities, at least as these are usually carried out. Women's organizations try to make it more possible for women to participate through advocating shared responsibility for child care and housework, affordable daycare of good quality, and by providing child care at meetings. Feminists have, in fact, changed our understanding of politics and of revolution. Radical activity heretofore has been defined as essentially male activity in the public realm, but it is now no longer understood in such limited and inaccurate ways.[29] Feminists have both brought the revolution home and taken women into the public sphere. The "personal is political" captures this shift in our notion of revolution, making it at once more personal and more everyday, at the same time connecting the everyday with social issues and entrenched structures of inequality. Politics occurs in the kitchen, the bedroom, the classroom, and the social work interview as well as in the legislature, law court, and boardroom. Again, perhaps one of the clearest examples of this is in the area of domestic violence. It is worth mentioning that many feminists object to the use of the term "domestic violence" because this obscures who is beating whom. Since the women's movement, a man beating his wife is no longer only a personal and private matter but also a public concern.

The Centrality of Relationships

The re-examination of theory/practice advocated here would necessarily involve a new look at relationships and communication, which are commonly understood to be central to social work. Such re-examination is complicated for women, including feminists, because women are heavily invested in relationships – having been socialized both as women and as social workers to be sensitive, caring, and giving and to do a disproportionate share of the work of maintaining relationships.

Traditional perspectives in social work emphasize relationship skills, but they do so out of the context of the inequality between worker and client. Practising empathy and warmth while remaining unaware of the structured inequalities in which social worker-client relations are embedded ends up being patronizing and manipulative. In my own student days, I was puzzled by the stress on human relations and communications.

If social workers valued humane and decent relations with clients, if these were fundamental to the delivery of counselling and other services, and if we spent so much time trying to teach and learn skills in relating and communicating, then, I used to wonder, how is it that clients often don't like social workers? The real function of the emphasis on relating to clients seems to mask the nature and severity of their problems and the depth and consequences of our own lack of understanding.

While dominant forms of social work prioritize relationships, implying that these occur in a social vacuum, early radical theory tended to dismiss relationships as tools to manipulate and coerce clients. Such an analysis was particularly difficult for women social workers because it attacked both what we believed was the heart of our professional practice and the basis of our socialized selves as women. Our essential value as social workers and as people was challenged.

In examining relationship skills and communication theories in a social context, feminist analysis of gender needs to be central. Shared reality and consciousness would become a basis for co-operative work – in contrast to professional-client, expert-recipient.

Conclusion

Except for the contributions of a few feminist social workers, the profession has yet to play a prominent part in the women's movement. While the profession embodies the contradictions and progressive themes in the larger society, on balance it reinforces rather than challenges dominant ideology. The profession has yet to confront an economic and political system that favours the interests of the powerful at the expense of those of the majority, particularly at the expense of the interests of oppressed groups, of which women are a large proportion. Social work is deeply enmeshed in the structures of inequality that exist in the wider world, including the inequality between women and men. The dominant models of theory and practice are inherently sexist and oppressive to women. In addition, social workers' location in government or government-funded agencies makes their participation in the struggle for women's equality very problematic.

Certainly, there have been important influences from the women's movement. Feminist analyses of gender, critiques of social policy, and information about alternative services for women are included in the curricula of most schools of social work. In larger cities, it is possible to find feminist counsellors and services, and more and more feminists are working in traditional social agencies. In spite of the increased awareness of inequality and oppression, significant changes in social policies and services and in agency and professional practices have yet to occur.

For social workers to participate fully in the feminist revolution, we will need to remake theory and practice, beginning with women and with feminist analyses of systemic inequalities. In building a new social work practice, a feminist practice means working collectively toward the empowerment of clients and social workers – toward the empowerment of women, since women form the majority of both groups. Methods of working collectively, however, will need to account for the realities of women's lives and those of direct service work, that is, the nature of the work, the crises, the pressures. Relationships between and among people will remain central, but these will be understood in the context of the wider world in which they take place – the world of grossly unequal power between women and men, poor and rich, black and white, and other whole groups of peoples. We will need to become more aware of how we are caught up in relations of domination and submission and of how to strive toward more equality in our relations with others. This is, of course, only one area where fundamental change is necessary, but it is an area of significance for social work and for women.

Feminists are attempting to do what has been suggested for social work – that is, feminists are taking into account systemic inequality and the exploitation and abuse of women, are accounting for this in their work in counselling and in providing services, and are attempting new ways of working together and new forms of helping that are empowering. No feminist claims that feminist counselling or community-based service alternatives are magic remedies for whatever ails women and society. Most of us have gone through enormous personal and professional struggles to shape our work more in accordance with our experience and developing analytical frameworks. Still, there is by now a considerable body of experience and theory that could be useful to social work education and the profession.

The women's movement has profoundly influenced people and social life and our conception of social change. We must now focus on creating the changes in the structures of power necessary for genuine equality and an end to oppression. If social workers make common cause with the feminist revolution in our time, then we can struggle together toward the freedom, justice, peace, and community for which we all long.

Notes

I thank Ben Carniol, Joan Cummings, Louise Dulude, Helen Levine, Roland Lecomte, Rick Williams, and Brian Wharf for their comments on earlier drafts of this chapter.

1. Social movements are generally defined as conscious, organized, and collective attempts to bring about large-scale changes in the social order. For an interesting discussion of social movements and specific protest movements, see Frances Fox Piven and Richard Cloward, *Poor People's Movements: Why They Succeed, How They Fail* (New York: Vintage Books, 1979).
2. For information about the women's movement in Canada, see Nancy Adamson, Linda Briskin, and Margaret McPhail, *Feminist Organizing For Change: The Contemporary Women's Movement in Canada* (Toronto: Oxford University Press, 1988); Catherine Cleverdon, *The Women's Suffrage Movement in Canada* (Toronto: University of Toronto Press, 1974); R. Cook and W. Mitchinson, eds., *The Proper Sphere: Women's Place in Canadian Society* (Toronto: Oxford University Press, 1976); Margrit Eichler and Marie Lavigne, "Women's Movement," in *The Canadian Encyclopedia* (Edmonton: Hurtig, 1985), pp. 1960–61; Angela R. Miles and Geraldine Finn, eds., *Feminism in Canada: From Pressure to Politics* (Montreal: Black Rose Books, 1982); Alison Pren-

tice *et al., Canadian Women: A History* (Toronto: Harcourt Brace Jova-
novich, 1988); Marylee Stephenson, *Women in Canada* (Toronto:
General Publishing, 1977); Lynne Teather, "The Feminist Mosaic,"
in Gwen Matheson, ed., *Women in the Canadian Mosaic* (Toronto:
Peter Martin Associates, 1976), pp. 301–46; S.J. Wilson, *Women, The
Family, and The Economy*, Second Edition (Toronto: McGraw-Hill
Ryerson, 1986).

3. In Canada, for example, women were granted the right to vote in
federal elections in 1918, and in most provinces between 1916 and
1922. Wilson, *Women, The Family, and The Economy*, pp. 130–34.

4. Joan E. Cummings discusses salary inequities between women and
men in social work in the Atlantic provinces and how these com-
pare with other occupational groups. See "Sexism in Social Work:
The Experience of Atlantic Social Work Women," *Atlantis*, 6, 2
(Spring, 1981), pp. 62–79.

5. Definitions of feminism and the women's movement can be found
in Cheris Kramarae and Paula A. Treichler, *A Feminist Dictionary*
(London: Pandora Press, 1985), pp. 158–61, 501–03.

6. Nancy Hartsock, "Feminist Theory and the Development of Revolutionary Strategy," in Zillah Eisenstein, ed., *Capitalist Patriarchy and
the Case for Socialist Feminism* (New York: Monthly Review Press,
1979), pp. 58–59.

7. Helen Levine, "Feminist Counselling – A Look at New Possibilities," *'76 and Beyond*, special issue of *The Social Worker*, Canadian
Association of Social Workers, 1976.

8. There are many excellent discussions of the range of theoretical
perspectives within feminism. See, for example, Bell Hooks, *Feminist
Theory: From Margin to Center* (Boston: South End Press, 1984); Alison
Jaggar, *Feminist Politics and Human Nature* (Totowa, N.J.: Rowman and
Allanheld, 1983); Juliet Mitchell and Ann Oakley, eds., *What is Femi-
nism: A Re-examination* (New York: Pantheon Books, 1986).

9. See Adrienne Rich, "Compulsory Heterosexuality and the Lesbian
Experience," *Signs: A Journal of Women and Society*, 5, 4 (Summer,
1980), pp. 631–60, for a discussion of how heterosexuality as an institution has been used to divide women and to re-enforce oppression
and lack of choice. hooks explores the limits of feminist theory and
practice in relation to black women and racism in *Feminist Theory*.

10. For a discussion of feminist criticisms of the traditional distinction
between subjectivity and objectivity, see Liz Stanley and Sue Wise,
Breaking Out: Feminist Consciousness and Feminist Research (London:
Routledge and Kegan Paul, 1983). Dorothy Smith shows how the

location of the "knower" in terms of social class, sex, race, time, and place shapes the knowledge created. She argues that separating knowledge from the people who produced it and the conditions and processes of their work results in theories that are harmful to women and other oppressed groups. Smith's work in developing a sociology for women has been recently collected and published in *The Everyday World as Problematic: A Feminist Sociology* (Toronto: University of Toronto Press, 1987).

11. For examples of traditional definitions of social work, see Dean H. Hepworth and JoAnn Larsen, *Direct Social Work Practice: Theory and Skills*, 2nd edition (Homewood, Ill.: The Dorsey Press, 1986); Louise C. Johnson, *Social Work Practice: A Generalist Approach* (Boston: Allyn and Bacon, 1983).

12. For useful discussion of social welfare policy and services under capitalist systems, see Jeffry H. Galper, *The Politics of Social Services* (Englewood Cliffs, N.J.: Prentice-Hall, 1975); Galper, *Social Work Practice: A Radical Perspective* (Englewood Cliffs, N.J.: Prentice-Hall, 1980); Paul Corrigan and Peter Leonard, *Social Work Practice Under Capitalism: A Marxist Approach* (London: Macmillan, 1978); Roy Bailey and Mike Brake, eds., *Radical Social Work* (New York: Pantheon, 1975). Ben Carniol, *Case Critical* (Toronto: Between the Lines, 1987), is a recent Canadian text that links the limitations in social services and social work practice to systemic inequalities in wealth and power.

13. These arguments have been made for many years and by many authors. See, for example, Leo Panitch, ed., *The Canadian State: Political Economy and Political Power* (Toronto: University of Toronto Press, 1977).

14. This understanding of the state comes from many sources. See, for example, London-Edinburgh Weekend Return Group, *In and Against the State* (London: Pluto Press, 1979).

15. Examples of feminist critiques can be found in the following: Mary Bricker-Jenkins and Nancy Hooyman, *Not For Women Only: Social Work Practice for a Feminist Future* (Silver Spring, Md.: NASW, 1986); Eve Brook and Ann Davis, *Women, the Family and Social Work* (London: Tavistock, 1985); Joan E. Cummings, "Sexism in Social Work: Some Thoughts on Strategy for Structural Change," *Catalyst: A Socialist Journal of the Social Services*, No. 8 (1980); Helen Levine, "The Personal Is Political," in Miles and Finn, eds., *Feminism in Canada*; Joan Turner and Lois Emery, eds., *Perspectives on Women in the 1980s* (Winnipeg: University of Manitoba Press, 1983); Mary Valentich,

"Feminism and Social Work Practice," in Joanne C. Turner and Francis J. Turner, eds., *Social Work Treatment* (New York: Free Press, 1979); Nan Van Den Bergh and Lynn B. Cooper, eds., *Feminist Visions for Social Work* (Silver Spring, Md.: NASW, 1986); Elizabeth Wilson, *Women and the Welfare State* (London: Tavistock, 1977); Elizabeth Wilson, "Feminism and Social Work," in Bailey and Brake, eds., *Radical Social Work* (London: E. Arnold, 1980).

16. Several analyses of Canada's political and economic structures point out the domination of government, business, professional, and other powerful interests by men who are rich or well connected to wealth, who are white, and who are often educated in law or business. See, in this regard, John Porter, *The Vertical Mosaic: An Analysis of Social Class and Power in Canada* (Toronto: University of Toronto Press, 1965); Wallace Clement, *The Canadian Corporate Elite: An Analysis of Economic Power* (Toronto: McClelland and Stewart, 1975).

17. Wilson, "Feminism and Social Work."

18. For a recent overview of poverty in Canada and its increasing concentration among women, see David P. Ross and Richard Shillington, *The Canadian Fact Book on Poverty, 1989* (Ottawa: Canadian Council on Social Development, 1989).

19. Barbara Blouin, with the support of The Women's Action Coalition of Nova Scotia, *Women and Children Last: Single Mothers on Welfare in Nova Scotia* (Halifax: Institute for the Study of Women, Mount Saint Vincent University, 1989).

20. This has been documented repeatedly. For recent studies from Nova Scotia, see *How Will the Poor Survive? A Discussion Paper on the Current Social Assistance System in Nova Scotia* (Halifax: Nova Scotia Association of Social Workers, 1987); *How Do the Poor Afford to Eat? An Examination of Social Assistance Food Rates in Nova Scotia* (Halifax: Nova Scotia Nutrition Council, 1988); *Report of the Task Force on Family and Children's Services* (Halifax: Nova Scotia Department of Community Services, 1987).

21. See Mary Schwartz, "Sexism in the Social Work Curriculum," *Journal of Education for Social Work*, 9, 3 (1973), pp. 65–70.

22. Adrienne Rich, *Of Woman Born: Motherhood as Experience and Institution*, Tenth Anniversary Edition (New York: W.W. Norton, 1986).

23. See, for example, Judith Myers Avis, "Deepening Awareness: A Private Study Guide to Feminism and Family Therapy," *Journal of Psychotherapy and the Family*, 3, 4 (Winter, 1987), pp. 15–46. This issue of the journal is entitled "Women, Feminism and Family Therapy."

24. Linda MacLeod, *Wife Battering in Canada: The Vicious Circle* (Ottawa: Canadian Advisory Council on the Status of Women, 1980); MacLeod, *Battered But Not Beaten: Preventing Wife Battering in Canada* (Ottawa: Canadian Advisory Council on the Status of Women, 1987).

25. For feminist counselling alternatives, see Miriam Greenspan, *A New Approach to Women and Therapy* (Toronto: McGraw-Hill Ryerson, 1983); Mary Russell, *Skills in Counselling Women – The Feminist Approach* (Springfield, Ill.: Charles C. Thomas, 1984). Service provision is discussed in Jillian Ridington, "Providing Services the Feminist Way," in Maureen FitzGerald, Connie Guberman, and Margie Wolfe, eds., *Still Ain't Satisfied: Canadian Feminism Today* (Toronto: The Women's Press, 1982).

26. For example, the inadequacies of welfare provisions in Nova Scotia have been documented in *How Will the Poor Survive?*

27. This and the following quotations are from feminist social workers interviewed for a study about the project of developing feminist practice.

28. Within the women's movement it is fairly often observed that transition houses are becoming more like traditional social agencies and that this is very much the consequence of government funding. Feminists who work in these houses or who serve on their boards and committees are faced with difficult choices. On the one hand, the service is needed and providing it requires government funds. On the other, seeking and obtaining government money means emphasizing the personal versus the social and political nature of the problem. Even fund-raising campaigns – for most transition houses raise a considerable proportion, often over one-third, of their operating capital by fund-raising – result in toning down the politics of battering. In fund-raising, it is sometimes suggested that the needs of the children be highlighted because the public tends to have more sympathy for children of battered women than for the women themselves.

29. Mary O'Brien discusses feminism and revolution in *The Politics of Revolution* (London: Routledge and Kegan Paul, 1981).

CHAPTER 4

Social Work and the First Nation Movement: "Our Children, Our Culture"

by Yvonne Howse and Harvey Stalwick

Introduction

Whom Do Social Workers Serve?

This blunt question, posed over fifty years ago by a leading social work educator and social reformer, Bertha Capen Reynolds, has considerable relevance for any discussion of social movements, social change, and the role of social workers.[1] The struggle and oppression experienced in the 1980s by Canadians of Native ancestry is starkly evident. The term "First Nation" has taken on an opposite meaning, for they are the last to enjoy any degree of twentieth-century equality. In this context we find Reynolds's answer to be challenging and specific to any understanding of the connection between social work and social movements: "Social Work exists to serve people in need. If it serves other classes who have other purposes, it becomes too dishonest to be capable of either theoretical or practical development."[2]

The social responsibility of being partisan, the act of taking sides with people in need, is the main theme of this chapter.

C. Wright Mills helps us understand ways to practise this value of participatory alignment when he describes the interplay between "private troubles" and "public issues." The specific meaning this holds for us is attention to ways people in need become agents of change – agents of transformation – by going beyond "personal troubles of milieu" when they become aware of "public issues of structure."[3]

That is, social work practice in the form of alignment actions shifts attention away from a blaming-the-victim model to examine critically larger economic and political issues such as social dislocation associated with racism and underdevelopment. Meaning is then provided for the inner life and external career of the individual[4] in the form of an activity where the person in need can intervene in and change aspects of the environment that have become a barrier.[5] Mills sees mass society as a major barrier where persons are "gripped by personal troubles which they are not able to turn into social issues."[6] For social workers involved with the First Nation movement, whether they are white or Native, the essential task of participatory alignment becomes one of building on Mills's belief so that the "personal is political."

Participatory alignment may not come easy given a history referred to by Mills as small-scale and small-minded social engineering forms of "liberal practicality" in a search for adaptation, adjustment, and, within the context of this chapter, assimilation to social framework.[7] In a devastating statement Mills describes social work as having an "occupationally trained incapacity to rise above a series of cases."[8] Clearly, any contemporary forms of social work practice that fail to go beyond this dismal pattern Mills portrayed in the 1940s and 1950s will certainly harm the integrity of the profession and possibly slow down the First Nation social movement. Some digging beneath the surface of this issue will reveal the extent of common ground shared by First Nation people and the profession of social work: "By and large social work values are congruent with Native values."[9]

However, as illustrated and discussed later in this chapter, the responsibility for putting an end to discrimination and all other barriers Native people experience should not be solely placed on the social worker and government official. More significantly, "the citizen must take the initiative, must set the course for the professional to follow, must provide the energy required for the social action program to effect permanent improvement."[10]

One opportunity for social workers and social work educators to decide which side they are on, and how they might work together with a social movement, is illustrated by the events of April, 1989, when First Nation people across Canada took a stand on treaty obligations and access to higher education. Many Natives protested; several went to jail charged with mischief for participating in the non-violent demonstrations at Department of Indian Affairs offices; and some fasted in a desperate attempt to challenge government policy. One Indian elder, speaking at a Regina demonstration, stated simply, "if we lose on education, we've lost it all."

These expressions of non-co-operation, passive resistance, and civil disobedience must be respected and cannot be blindly overlooked by the social work profession. In the same way, the apparent breakdown of constitutional negotiations regarding self-government, the Meech Lake Accord, and the fact aboriginal people do not have many ways to participate in government through the electoral system should be heeded by a profession that had its roots in human rights struggles to make the democratic process serve people in need.

The issue of entitlement to education and the rapidly emerging expression of self-governing through control over the delivery of child welfare and family support services as a means of regaining "our children and our culture" combine to set an agenda in the 1990s for social workers open to becoming aligned with the First Nation social movement. For such a working together to be honest and capable of theoretical and practical development, hard questions need to be answered by all concerned persons.

Posing Questions Assists Social Movement

The posing of questions, over the centuries, has been at the heart of dialogue leading to new knowledge and action. For

Paulo Freire and other popular educators, the steps are action-filled: "One must not transform the world (reality) without transforming the consciences of persons ... the processes are dialectic, contradictory, in process."[11] The stakes are high and reflect a political commitment to the transformation of an unjust society.

This commitment is related to questions about the good life; how the actual and the possible are not the same; and how individuals can struggle to change the world.[12] Such a perspective is found in the following definition of empowerment: " ... an interactive process involving mutual respect and critical reflection through which both people and controlling institutions are changed in ways that provide those people with greater influence over individuals and institutions which are in some way impeding their efforts to achieve equal status in society, for themselves and those they care about."[13]

Strategies for Social Change: Reflection and Action

The real achievements of posing the right questions and of gaining empowerment do not come in one day. There is no quick cure for "not knowing" and inaction. A critical reading of the dialogue-conversation in the next section of this chapter upholds this view and suggests the need for strategies by social workers and educators to deal with the challenge of forming participatory alignments. The following questions provide a working connection between the practice of social work and social movements based on reflection and action.

How is it possible to revive in social workers a sense of citizenship duties and citizen-led movements that feature participatory democracy? For example, this could be expressed in terms of civil rights issues. In 1948, a social work philosopher, Eduard C. Lindeman, wrote:

As citizen, as humanitarian, as technician and as social scientist social workers share a distinct responsibility to the question of civil rights, both with respect to its specific incidents and its comprehensive meaning. I cannot conceive of a bona fide social worker who could remain aloof from this cause and still think of himself as having fulfilled his professional responsibilities, to say nothing of duties as a citizen.[14]

Lindeman summed up the social workers' task as "to bring freedom to the person in need, to reveal to him the methods by which he can free himself of his burden and thus regain his sense of dignity."[15]

How is it possible to seek a Native-defined future in place of integration, assimilation, or some other programs conceived by whites? For a start, efforts should be taken by non-racists to confront the white backlash to Native advancement so that social changes will not be eroded. Issues such as racism need to be named so that forms of anti-racist social work practice and policies may be developed by the professional community.[16] For example, advocacy/empowerment skills could include partisan participatory action research, social leadership development, and political education. Once the social work field is organized around such issues, systematic efforts should be undertaken by social workers to align and co-operate with client-advocacy groups and representatives of Native social movements.[17]

How common is the perception that social workers are concerned only with personal services within the confines of the agency to the exclusion of attention to social circumstances, social policies, and damaging attitudes in society such as blaming the victim and racism? Does this perception alarm the professional community as representing forms of bad social work lacking a service ethic and collective effort to improve the quality of life? That is, there is a need to develop an awareness of how clinical intervention could go beyond the superficial when factors such as poverty, unemployment, housing, and racism are recognized less as individual personal problems and more as public issues and massive social problems. In this regard, the "personal is political" aspect of feminist social work practice, as discussed elsewhere in this book, has much to offer as a theoretically grounded response.

How should the Canadian Association of Social Workers' Code of Ethics be revised to place more emphasis on critical awareness, empowerment, and participatory action research skills for practitioners and clients? Progressive social workers should ensure that their ideology is compatible with the general aims of advancing the Native social movement.[18] Part of this compatibility could feature an affirming of ethical standards of caring now present and being developed within Native-controlled human services.

A relevant question to address during these neo-conservative times is, how should the idea of freedom be expressed in a Native-directed social movement and in the actions of progressive social workers? Bertha Capen Reynolds wrote in the preamble to a 1948 poem: "Know what you fear, and why. Loss of our liberties is an imminent threat, only to be averted by a people who care enough, and dare to be angry – by a people that can put aside minor differences and unite. The labour movement did not learn this lesson through many bitter years."

> Freedom is a dear-bought thing
> but not so costly as chains.
>
> What do we fear to lose?
> Our privileges or our liberties?
> Privileges at whose expense?
>
> Liberty for what and for whom?
> What power do we dread?
> Arms, or lying tongues,
> Or food withheld?
> Helpless, all of them,
> Against the wrath of a people
> That knows its own united strength.[19]

However, the most fundamental question is, who should speak about Native persons' oppression and related social movement experiences? When such words come only from outsiders it could block a much-needed rereading of history for such a social movement. This danger is expressed by Gustavo Gutierrez:

The history of humanity has been written "with a white hand" from the side of the dominators. History's losers have another outlook. History must be read from a point of departure in their struggles, their resistance, their hopes. Many an effort has been made to blot out the memory of the oppressed and thereby deprive them of a source of energy, of historical will, of rebellion. Today down-trodden peoples seek to comprehend their past in order to build their present on solid foundations.[20]

The answer suggested by Gutierrez is to see events, which in the context of this chapter would refer to Native persons' social movement, through the eyes of those who are experiencing oppression. This search for authentic voices is essential in any attempt to answer the question, who should speak? On this point Gutierrez observes: "We shall not have our great leap forward ... until the marginalized and exploited have begun to become the artisans of their own liberation – until their voice makes itself heard directly, without mediations, without interpreters. . . . "[21]

His challenge to find ways to make it possible for oppressed people to be heard directly is echoed in the views of Simone Weil, who asked people she respected: "What are you going through?" For her, the capacity to hear required a special form of concentration, a true attention consisting of: "suspending our thought, leaving it detached, empty and ready to be penetrated ... waiting, not seeking anything, but ready to receive the object in its naked truth."[22] This challenge of Gutierrez and the penetrating insight of Weil contribute to a quality of relationships essential for persons seeking to bring about social change.

Respect for persons' experience and the empowerment such an expression has in the formation of movements for social change are clearly reflected in the life and work of Paulo Freire. Writing about this process, he states: "only the oppressed, as the social class that has been forbidden to speak, can become the utopians, the prophets and the messengers of hope, provided that their future is not simply a reformed repetition of the present. Their future is the realization of the liberation – without which they cannot be."[23]

Does respect for this process allow any room for action by social workers interested in the social change objectives of the

First Nation social movement? Should they back off? At the 1985 Dialogue on Strategies for Change in Social Work Education conference held at the University of Regina,[24] this question was answered by Chief Angus McLean of the James Smith Cree Nation: "I'll say this to the professors, the institutions and to those that are servicing our people out in the field ... 'backing off' is not good enough. Get in there and help."[25] Clearly, the most helpful process will be one that returns power to people in the midst of realizing change. Such a process is reviewed in an International Association of Schools of Social Work survey of indigenous social work methodology. The University of Massey in New Zealand and the University of Regina Taking Control Project were cited as two examples of "returning power to the Native culture ... and empowering people to direct their own social services needs and delivery."[26] Other examples included the University of Papua, New Guinea, social research institutes in India and the Philippines, and Latin America, where a movement away from colonial influences, the process of "conscientization," and a focus on community development directed by local people based on specific cultural frameworks were viewed by this survey as "the beginning of direct involvement in the people's struggle for total human development."[27]

Bertha Reynolds's view of social work as existing to serve people in need urges that social workers should "get in there and help."[28] Direction on how to help is suggested by Freire:

First, by claiming that neutrality of action cannot exist and by refusing to administer to individuals or groups or communities through purely anesthetic forms of action, the social worker who opts for change strives to unveil reality. She or he works with, never on, people whom she or he considers subjects, not objects or incidences, of action. As one who is humble and critical, she or he cannot accept the ingenuity embodied in the 'ready-made idea' generalized in such a way that the social worker appears as the 'agent of change'. This act of refusal is not just for some of us but for all who are committed to change.[29]

Our bias, as indicated above, is consistent with what we understand to be the intention of Frances Fox Piven and Richard Cloward in *Poor People's Movements* when they refer to bringing people fully into history, "not simply as victims but as actors."[30] To this end we rely on voices becoming text to avoid a form of writing that "displaces the subject from the world."[31] The following dialogue-conversation between the authors focuses on aspects of social movement building in the area of Native child welfare and family support alternatives and on experiences of Native women in the midst of a struggle to realize a vision of "our children, our culture."[32] Some of the issues and topics discussed include: generational deprivation syndrome, cultural genocide, racism, classism, colonization, dynamics of separation, searching for roots, and how shared stories of survival empower people.

In our view, the process of dialogue-conversations among First Nation persons, progressive social workers, educators, and others involved in social movement offers promise as a means of critical self-examination and as a major catalyst for social change.[33] Such a process of authentic mutual learning has yet to happen in a universal way in Canada. When the level of dialogue is raised to the consideration of principles, values, and belief systems,[34] we are confident that the central purpose of this book will be realized. That is, the process of participatory alignment and liberating learning will then reach deeper into an understanding of the objectives of First Nation social movement, will respect the contributions of this movement's experience in reshaping a philosophy of social work, and will assist in creating a model of social work that willingly turns its back on social control and defends the authentic serving of people in need.

Dialogue-Conversation: "A Cultural Perspective, Yesterday/Today"

HARVEY: On the topic of social movements and people making changes to overcome conditions that keep them oppressed, where should we begin?

YVONNE: I would really like everyone to have open minds to be able to understand what has occurred with our people. Then maybe we won't be so judgemental of our own people and people that we see suffering. The most painful thing with our people is watching them destroy one another, watching them judge one another and be judged. We don't need that within our society: *that has been planned for us*. We have to understand what that plan was. We need to understand what has happened in terms of our divisions, in terms of the patterns of deprivation, and in terms of racism. Part of what I call *this plan* is called cultural genocide. This is a perspective from myself and from other First Nation people. I have listened to the horror stories that they have gone through.

HARVEY: You mention divisions. An old saying, "divide and rule," with the powerful maintaining power, is one form of oppression. Is this what you mean?

Overcoming Divisions in Our lives

YVONNE: Divisions within our people have happened. I look back to when I was twenty years old (I'm forty now) and I think of when my daughter wasn't born yet. I was involved with what was called the Fred Quilt Committee – that was about a First Nation man in British Columbia who was killed by the RCMP and we challenged them. I remember, at that time, saying to people I was involved with that if we are going to make changes we have to be strong enough to make those changes. I remember being interviewed at that time and they asked me, "Are you treaty, Métis, or non-status?"

People have to look at that. The divisions within our nation start from there. It wasn't us – it wasn't our ancestors who defined us as treaty, Métis, and non-status – it was not them. It was colonization through the Indian Act that defined who was treaty. And where did that come from? It came from the government of the day. That is where it came from.

HARVEY: You link these divisions with racism?

YVONNE: Yes. Why is it that in 1990 I still have to discuss racism, not just within my family system, but outside of it as well? How many people are we going to allow to be destroyed? How many children are going to be dead before we wake up? Before we say "that's enough, I've had it." There is nothing the matter with challenging people.

My kids go to school. The toughest decision in my life was to put my daughter, my youngest one, in school. I knew racism was there. I knew it wasn't going to change by the time she got to school. I knew that. I didn't want her to suffer because she is a Cree-Ojibway child. She is handling it pretty good. Sometimes she says, "Mom, I don't think those teachers like us because they continuously pick out and shame Native kids."

Oppression: Learning Who Is Our Enemy

HARVEY: Yvonne, from our work together I know you see and live the importance of dialogue in many areas where change is needed. Out of such straight talk and critical thinking change is often possible. Paulo Freire speaks of "naming" what is wrong as part of this process of reflecting, saying "what ought to be" and then acting.

YVONNE: We need to name our oppressor. The oppression of the people starts very consciously. For some people, who are the oppressed, they are not fully aware of how they, too, can become the oppressor. Oppression means you keep a people down or you control a people in a certain manner. Governments control by dollars. Employers and bosses control. The oppression of our people, in terms of the larger context of looking at oppression, started with ways to industrialize our people, including assimilation and detribalization. We know that not long after the treaties were signed, whites were already trying to figure a way to get rid of a people, to liquidate them. There was actually a plan called the liquidation plan.[35] To liquidate Indians' culture. That actually existed and still does through the child welfare system.

Within our nation, it's hard to look out and see who is the enemy, who in heaven's name is the enemy? Is it my next door neighbour or is it the guy that lives two miles away from me, or is it the everyday white person that I see? *This white system is the actual enemy.* Our people have to understand that system to beat that system. *We have to beat it.* We can't continue to allow the destruction of our people to occur. Otherwise we are not going to have any nations. The master plan of cultural genocide that was developed will occur if we don't do something about it ourselves now.

There is a master plan of cultural genocide and I can't look at it any differently.[36] Whether people agree or disagree, that is what has occurred. Consciously or unconsciously, it happened and still does happen. We're going back in time for our analysis because you have to go back in order to understand where we are today. In terms of looking at it as to what is happening and what has happened to our children and what happened to our people and generations of all of our people, we have to go back and learn from the past. We have to look at it, we have to understand it.

A letter sent to the East, from a northern Saskatchewan missionary in 1874, refers to detribalization. We know all of that was planned in the 1830s and how policies of "civilization" came out of that process.[37] He sent this letter back to Montreal saying, "The only way we can civilize these people is to remove their children." That's fact, that's history, that was done. At the end of the letter he also wrote, "I don't know if what we are doing to these people is right." So he, no doubt, at one point had some sort of consciousness of what he was doing and what was being planned, but never to excuse him. I wish that I would have been there in 1874! Maybe we would have been able to stop some of the pain and sorrow our people have gone through and are still going through.

HARVEY: It would seem that total institutions came into existence as part of a total solution for "the Native problem." This has contributed to what you often refer to as deprivation rates. What do you mean? What have been some of your experiences with institutions?

YVONNE: We're looking strongly at deprivation rates – deprivation rates within our people because of institutionalization. What happens when you institutionalize? What happens if I decided today to take Native children from their parents and bring them into an institution and then hire a few priests and a few nuns to educate and assimilate these kids so that they can behave in a manner that they wanted them to behave, not what Native people want? When the children get older they have been deprived of adequate parenting skills, because when in an institution there is not a natural parent-child relationship. I was in an institution, I know what institutions are like. There were 250 of us sitting there and eating, with nuns walking around making sure we're "eating properly." A young girl, who would have an epileptic fit, would get a good licking. I shouldn't say good, because it was a wicked licking. Institutionalization has occurred and caused deprivation.

I know that from the time when one is small and, as you grow, how those deprivation patterns develop. There was a routine with someone always feeding you because we didn't have to cook in the convent. I didn't have to cook in the convent, not at all. I didn't even know how to boil water! They didn't teach us anything in there. All I knew was that Mass. I knew Latin – how to say Mass in Latin, how to answer it in Latin, because that's what I was taught. I could have fallen into that same pattern of deprivation if it wasn't for people that I met that I could sit and talk with. These people were aware of what happened to our people in this country. I was one who was fairly lucky. I was one who was also able to meet elders who were not in the system, who didn't even understand from personal experience what the boarding school was all about. But they knew institutionalization destroyed a lot of people.

HARVEY: What do you mean by "destroyed a lot of people"?

YVONNE: For example, look at the Lebret residential school in Saskatchewan, which was built over a hundred years ago by Catholic missionaries. This is one example of free education as promised to all who signed treaties and to all their descendants. In one of the treaties it stated: "The Queen wishes her red children to learn the cunning of the white man and when they are ready for it, she will send school masters." The Queen certainly did do that! We also know Lebret was called an industrial school and this was a "good name" because the name industrial school means we became the "industry" for others. It was a good plan for them, but not such a good plan for us! There were also other ways to destroy us.

We're also looking at the time of reservations and the pain and the suffering that happened on those reservations. They, too, became a form of institutionalization and cause of deprivation patterns: the starvation that went on, the cards, the licence and the passes an Indian had to have from the Indian agent in order to leave that reservation. The land is all that we had and there was very little of it. Not to put down the reservations, but that's all that's there. The reality of developing the reservations was to destroy a people: you keep a people ignorant by keeping a people away from learning and denying them what most citizens in this country ever had. By keeping them away you isolate them from the rest of society in the same way industrial schools, convents, and reservations kept us separate. That's what the annihilation plan imposed on us has done.

The deprivation patterns caused by the institutionalization of our children has gone on for five generations. We're still doing it in Saskatchewan. We still have children in care – we have over 330 children in an Indian-controlled boarding school in Prince Albert.[38] I don't know how many children they have in Lebret. So we haven't stopped it. It's still going on. We're still institutionalizing at the fifth generation.

Indian People in Jail

HARVEY: Are there some other examples of institutionalization and patterns of deprivation?

YVONNE: Let's see what's happening in Prince Albert at the Pine Grove jail for women. It starts back with the industrial schools and how our people have those deprivation patterns developed that result in perpetuation of the rest of the system, including the child welfare system. You go to Pine Grove and you will see that 100 per cent of the women in jail are aboriginal women. I get calls from those women – they say, "Yvonne, will you help me get my kids?" I'm never going to turn down a mother who wants her children. We have to stop and look at the institutional process and understand it.

When we look at Pine Grove, how many of our women are in there for serious crimes? A lot of them are petty crimes. But they are in there. You can go to Pine Grove and can sit with the women and ask, "Were you at home, or were you in boarding school? Was your mother at home, or was your mother in boarding school, or in the industrial school?" Nine times out of ten, they will tell you, "I was in the boarding school, my mother was in the boarding school, my grandma was in the boarding school, my grandmother's mother was in the boarding school." What does that tell you? What does that say?

It says that generation after generation, because of the lack of the parenting within the home and because our kids could not stay home, they were sent to the boarding school. They were not parented. That dependency of the meals and of somebody looking after you (they really don't take care of you) doesn't make you feel like you are the most precious human being in the world. Our women are in there because of this plan of cultural genocide. Society will say, "Well, they pulled a B&E (breaking and entering). What are we supposed to do? Just let them get away with it?" Blame the victims, that's all it is. Nothing more.

The plan of the assimilation and industrialization of our people is also clear when you can go to the penitentiary where you will see our men. You can go to the Prince Albert correctional centre or the one in Regina and who do you see? Go to the boys' school, who do you see? Ask Saskatchewan Social Services what percentage of kids in care are of Indian ancestry? Well, I'll tell you, 48 per cent we know are treaty. That's a high percentage. We know that because of the bill-back system of the federal government – payment from the feds to the province. But we do not know the number or the percentage of children in care who are Métis children, mainly because the present data collection system refuses to get this information. We believe there has to be anywhere from 15 to 20 per cent who are Métis. So we look at the number of children within that system as amounting to at least 68 per cent of the total number of children in care. This is 1990, for goodness sakes. Those are 1987 statistics. The industry of our children is very much in practice and still exists within the provincial system.

Racism and Classism

HARVEY: Earlier you said we haven't cleared up racism. Why does it continue?

YVONNE: So some whites can keep their jobs! To survive they

need a race of people to exploit – someone else to do the low, menial jobs. They have lived off the backs of the people, of First Nation people, for too long. Other people in this country want to work with us. A few are and we respect them. When the few become many, then some of this fog of racism will lift. Racism has to be unlearned and good learning comes from people, First Nation people and all other people, thinking and acting together.

HARVEY: How does what you say about jobs and racism apply to people who are in jails?

YVONNE: Pine Grove is 100 per cent First Nation women inmates – I used to say 90 per cent until I went and had dinner with them. I was looking to see where were the non-Native women inmates? The only other women sitting there were the non-Native guards. Go to the penitentiary and jails for men in western Canada and you will see the same picture – guards, teachers, and cooks are all white.

The other thing we need to take a look at is the classism that we live with within this society. There is no sense to say it does not exist, because it does. Who decides what can happen with my life, my children, our societies? The Minister of Indian Affairs! The Minister is at the district office today. I wish I would have been able to go there and tell him, "You know nothing about our people. The money doesn't touch the reservations. I'll tell you we are lucky if they get five cents on the dollar. We are just trying to survive." It would be nice if we could get the funds and develop the programs the way they should be – that is, not keeping people down and sick. We would be in that job class that is interested in making people healthy – and, we would, if we had those jobs!

I spent a lot of time listening to other women, who have lived twenty, thirty, forty years longer than I have, talk about what it was like in the 1920s. The pain and the horror that comes from them is terrible. It is no wonder children were lost. It is certainly clear the society, at that time, didn't go back and look at what they were doing. Later, many people, including the social workers that participated in the damaging of our people by removing our children, were like puppets. They were part of that process without understanding. You don't take that in the school of social work. When you talk about what has occurred with our people – people don't want to listen all that well. They don't want to hear. They say, "Oh, well, that was yesterday: good grief, Yvonne, that was in the 1800s." What's different today? One difference now is that First Nation people are doing it to other First Nation people. We sure learned the cunning of the white man!

HARVEY: In 1985 both of us attended a workshop with Paulo Freire and we had a long, memorable visit with Paulo and his wife Elsa. At that time you shared stories of Native women and children, explaining the situation you are now discussing. I recall how shocked both were, especially Elsa. It was a moving experience to feel their concern and understanding. They were allies providing encouragement and asking about what changes are possible. What changes are taking place?

YVONNE: I remember that beautiful visit and Elsa's concern. To some extent First Nation child welfare groups have taken control, but it's not total control of their child welfare systems since these groups have to work within existing provincial child welfare acts. In Manitoba the way to increase dollars for children is to apprehend them. Apprehend means you take and remove the kids. It's the same here in Saskatchewan. How are you going to keep the system and people going? Easy, you apprehend the children and then you get the money. As a result there is very little money available to avoid apprehension, support families, and consider forms of prevention.

Our History, Our Healing

HARVEY: In the supportive awareness work you and others in Peyakowak (They Are Alone) do with persons returning after being "away" because of adoption or foster home or institutional placement, I have observed how care is taken to explain patiently the history of oppression, the dynamics of separation and being reunited with extended family and biological roots. As a result, some dramatic understandings begin in the lives of persons who, in their confusion and anger, had nearly reached the end of their rope. In this way, history becomes healing once people *know* their situation.

YVONNE: Part of the dynamics of separation is that we are looking at hurt and we are looking at pain. Separation is like a death. Death means not only to go and be sad but there is also a tremendous amount of anger experienced by the loved ones who are still behind. "How dare they die on me?" can be a question, depending on what happened in terms of the death. Those are the same things that are occurring with children when we remove them so readily. We don't stop to think of the hurt that we are putting the children through. A friend of mine once said, "You know, Yvonne, the crying will come before the anger." That's true, when you observe and participate in the reuniting of a family.

We feel guilty about death, too. We may say, if only I would have done that or maybe if I would have done this, maybe that person would not have died. The verbal stages of the young people who can express their pain are important to recognize. We sometimes limit them because we don't want to deal with it ourselves.

We don't have control over life, over the destiny of any one human being, or even of ourselves. But we do have some control now. If we are returning children let's develop all the necessary support systems to do so.

We have to have something that will make the difference for those kids and for the families that adopted the children and definitely for the families that have lost the children. We need to develop support groups, we need to develop ways of welcoming them home – because institutions are not where they should be returning.

HARVEY: What are some recent experiences you have had with persons returning?

YVONNE: For example, Peyakowak had the recent experience of bringing people back from the United States after many years in adoption and foster home placements. While this was a great time for the extended family when the daughter came back, I could see how she felt in terms of her displacement. Because she was displaced. Where was she to go? How do you go to live with your family who is now living in poverty? How do you come from the white middle-class system? That is, how can you come from a $100,000 home and move into a $10,000 home? You move into the home and there is no phone – all the conveniences we take for granted may not be there. This young lady from the States is coming home thinking she is going to live in a mansion. She didn't.

Another recent experience of reuniting someone after being adopted was one from Louisiana. The same process – her own stereotyping of her own people. She is still trying to work it out with her extended family, with her sisters and her brothers. She still has two brothers in Louisiana, who were adopted out of Saskatchewan. She came from Baton Rouge, Louisiana, with a southern drawl. So it was quite difficult for her and it still is. We don't have a welcoming halfway place to put them so that intensive treatment of what needs to be done can be done. We don't have that.

"I Am Not Going To Oppress Others"

HARVEY: How can social workers and other concerned persons be most helpful in the areas you wish to see changed?

YVONNE: Society can't continue to destroy people because it feels it has control. Social workers may not be aware of their own oppression and how they oppress clients. They do, very readily, unless they make a conscious commitment saying: "I am not going to oppress others." One has to make that commitment consciously. One cannot unconsciously continue to go around saying "I don't know." It is important to know – to make it conscious. Become aware of how displaced children become victims of the larger society. Don't destroy families, support them.

Society has these children and we know that 68 per cent in Saskatchewan are gone from First Nation homes, from our families and our communities. They know that this percentage of our future is lost. Now how are social workers going to work it out, or deal with, or support and help these children who are already suffering? Let's leave the mammas and the papas with some dignity. Let's not scoop up kids as readily as we have in the past.

Let's look for the extended family. Let's look for the support that Native families need to keep their children. This government is spending so much money keeping kids away from home. Think of how they could have put that money within the home, within the family system to strengthen the kids at home. That would have been far cheaper than removing the child.

HARVEY: What specific questions and issues should be considered by social workers involved in child welfare and family support services?

YVONNE: Our kids are coming back, what can we do with them? What can we do with the adoptive parents? How can we convince them that we are not going to just run in and steal all these kids? We are going to have to go through a human process to help those kids to get back and be stabilized with their own family system. They need to come back to human beings who care. White social workers have to know all those different things about the Native families and the kids before we go and just klunk them in and say, "Well, I'm glad you met your ma and pa, good for you," and not see them again and not know what's happening when the social worker leaves.

We, as First Nation people, know the dynamics of separation for the child. It is the same for the mom and the same for the pa, the grandparents, and the whole community. I know that if our fourteen-year-old boy is saying: "No, I don't want to meet my mom, she gave me up, she doesn't love me, she doesn't want me," what the kid really is saying is: "I'm scared that they are going to say that they don't want me again." Social service workers interpret that to mean the kid does not want anything to do with its parents. That is not right. That kid is saying to you, "I'm scared." That feeling of rejection is still there. Who wants to be rejected? Look at that child. If that child was taken before the verbal stage, that child does not have the words to explain what he or she feels. The feeling of rejection is there and there is fear. It's very real for them. So we have to understand all of that.

I've had white worker after white worker say to me, "What would happen if that kid does not want to meet his parents?" I say, "What was the child told about his family?"

Sometimes social workers may say to a child, "I know you want to stay with your mom but your mom can't take care of you right now." Maybe they don't say that – maybe they say, "Your mom's a drunk and she doesn't want you." I know we have to work, support, and care for each other differently from what we have been doing. All systems must become different and develop human ways of caring, truly caring.

Shared Stories of Survival

HARVEY: In our work together on the Taking Control Project we have collected the stories of many First Nation persons. The sharing of their stories empowers, builds movements, and contributes to a fighting literature as described by Franz Fanon. For him this literature expresses the heart of the people and becomes "the mouthpiece of a new reality in action."[39] In a similar way your personal story of survival has given hope to many.

YVONNE: I survived that child welfare system – with a little help from my friends! I feel even sorrier for the white child because I don't hear groups pulling together and saying, "What is happening now to all children has to stop." However, I hear groups saying that within our First Nations. I pity the lonely white child caught in the child welfare system because nobody is standing up for him. Everybody is collaborating and helping to destroy that child, too. So the patterns of deprivation are there and they become the oppression of a people. When a people, time after time, are oppressed they have to stand up and say, "That's enough." Our people are beginning to get the strength that we once had to be able to do that.

Escape from Reform

Paulo Freire has said: "The reform can clarify the exploitive nature of the situation and instead of making people docile it can awaken the people. Once reform starts it can escape from the hands of those who started it and provoke transformation."[40] Reform in the past has tragically stood in the way of a First Nation vision of mending and restoring "our children, our culture." In the 1980s this vision stood as one of several social movement forces, including the 1982 Canadian Constitution Act rights for Indian, Métis, and Inuit persons; treaty-affirmed land rights; and the transfer of economic, educational, social, and health institutions as part of the inherent right of Indian government.[41] The remark is often made, "What is the point of everything we are struggling for if we have not cared for our children, the seeds of future generations?" Does this vision match the action of an "unalterable course directed to the transfer of all child welfare matters from general agencies into the hands of Indian, Métis or Inuit communities"?[42] There is momentum for change.

The present reform, as illustrated by the development of Indian Child and Family Services (ICFS) in Canada, deserves critical study. It provides a lens through which to see issues more clearly and, as Paulo Freire observes, to "clarify the exploitive nature of the situation." A limited synopsis of a complex development riddled with years of protracted and often bitter negotiations among federal and provincial governments and Indian organizations is found in a recent Native Council of Canada report on child care.

> Apart from the quality of what has happened, the quantity of activity regarding the Department of Indian Affairs and Northern Development (DIAND) supported ICFS services in Canada is both remarkable and, for some, alarming. By 1986 55 percent of the 565 bands in Canada had service agreements representing an increase of 400 percent in five years in the numbers of bands enabled to deliver some or all of the services included under child welfare. For 21 percent of all bands this meant full control of all services delivered to their members. . . . As an economic and employment strategy this pace of activity stimulated the creation of new, but usually low paid, service sector jobs for Indian people and represented some shift in the flow of child welfare dollars and control from provincial sources to the Indian community.[43]

The Department of Indian Affairs and Northern Development noted that "Band directed community care contrasts markedly with provincial child welfare services in reducing the number of children in care ... and providing a focus on the family as a whole."[44] However, as the Native Council of Canada indicated, "This activity was regarded by politicians and civil servants as being too costly – there had been a doubling from $35 million to $70 million in five years and by 1989 costs had almost tripled."[45]

A concern with increased expenditures outweighed the positive results of Native-controlled child welfare. After 1986 the federal government refused to negotiate any further Indian Child and Family Services agreements with bands in Canada, a likely result of a 500+-page report from the cost-cutting Nielsen Task Force on Program Review titled *Improved Program Delivery: Indians and Natives*.[46] As the Native Council indicated, "This high profile zealous 'bottom line' effort to reduce federal expenditure also contained the disturbing (disturbing for Indian persons) philosophy of devolution of federal obligations to provincial administration."[47]

In discussing the reform of recent years, the Council implied the difficulty inherent in the reform process becoming social movement:

> The attention during the past decade of ICFS reform activity, directed as it is to the on-reserve population, has diverted public ... attention from the needs of off-reserve and urban Native children and families. This 'invisible' population is estimated to be 750,000 – twice the on-reserve population. ... As reported on the Task Force on Child Care, Native families who are not on reserves need good child care, to allow parents to seek and maintain gainful employment, and to facilitate cultural adjustment of the non-Native environments, at the same time providing the opportunity for them to preserve and maintain their language and cultural tradition.[48]

We are left to ponder: when is reform a hindrance in the advancement of social movement? In what ways can reform be helpful? When does reform escape from the hands of those who started it?

The central issue in the present reform appears to be a lingering of the old issue of whether or not politicians, civil servants, social policy-makers, and citizens are able fully to turn away from a set of "liberal practicality" assimilation values and celebrate the value of cultural differences – in effect, to embrace "radical culture theories" that maintain that each culture must be understood in terms of its own system of meaning and action.[49] Optimism that this reform will be helpful in this way is seen in terms of attention given to establishing Indian standards for services. The potential exists to codify traditional and preferred practices. To what extent this will be funded adequately and be part of a community-based participatory research approach remains to be determined.

Other positive results of the ICFS reform are the empowering opportunities it provides for local organizing, where individuals are taking action on what is vital and deeply imbedded in the culture. The experience of taking control of "our lives, our children, our culture" means that other opportunities for self-determination will follow in the future, with the focus on how the "personal is political." This reform process can awaken people to ask questions about social issues, such as the need for an adequate economic base for full and satisfying employment. Such questions go well beyond "personal troubles" and give people hope of linking up with a better social life.

This reform can also help establish, in the words of Myles Horton, "alternate approaches by Indian people as being superior, not inferior, because they are different."[50] For this to happen, however, the corner needs to be turned on the view that provincial child welfare and family services legislation is a repository of years of experience and knowledge that should not be displaced[51] with an alternate legal framework within the context of Indian government. Support for this to happen will come from social workers who come to realize that much of past and present social work practice with Native families is bad practice – with the best of intent it has destroyed families. Dialogue is one way of empowering people to name their oppressors, to expose conditions and take this necessary first step in freeing all people, social workers included, to connect personal troubles with social issues. Social workers must also acknowledge that while most Indian families are oppressed and poor, they have the power within to affect the direction of their lives. It seems to us that this is the reality that must be described because – to follow an old social work dictum of beginning where the client is – only as this reality is recognized and dealt with will there be any prospect for change.

Our experience with ICFS reform attempts and our direct involvement with Peyakowak (They Are Alone) in Saskatchewan as an alternative Native family support program help "clarify" the oppressed state of Indian families and the damage that has and is being caused by social workers and social welfare organizations. It is imperative that social workers learn about power, its impact, and how it can oppress. Social work education has largely ignored the consequences of the exercise of power, and, given the amount of power vested in social workers in such fields of service as child welfare and mental health, this ignorance is inexcusable. Case studies of Indian families and their history in their own words would provide valuable insights into the impact of power exercised without reference to the culture and values of Native people. For example, we need to understand contradictions apparent in the self-serving pretence of social workers who believe it is possible to "heal" within a context where social purposes are connected to social control.[52]

Paulo Freire reminds us that "Once reform starts it can escape from the hands of those who started it and provoke transformation." Based on our research, this appears to be an accurate anticipation of the direction ICFS reform will take in the 1990s. Assisting this escape are participatory research as a means to "validate people's perception of their reality"[53] and the growing group of experience-educated, well-qualified Native persons entering once-denied social leadership roles. A participatory research evaluation of the alternative family-centred and community-based approach of the Champagne/Aishihik Child Welfare Project in the Yukon is one example of participatory alignments among concerned persons who respect a culture and its reality.[54] While respecting clients and their right to self-determination is a cardinal principle in social work practice, it has all too often not been honoured where minority groups are concerned. When social work practice and child-care programs are built on Native values and traditions the results are impressive. We strongly favour First Nation control of child welfare programs, but only if these are transformed into programs that support families and communities.

For an escape from reform to happen so as to "provoke transformation," barriers to social change need to be considered. Barriers or hindrances include those features of reform that stand in the way of realizing the original vision. One negative result can be an illusion of change followed by a sense of having been deceived. Ron Lewis, former director of the Social Work Program of the Saskatchewan Indian Federated College, has stated:

> I can tell you what is going to happen if we imitate the same programs that we have. Indian people are going to be tremendously upset . . . to see these kinds of programs headed by Indians who haven't come up with new ideals, who haven't blended the culture, who haven't had the courage to say "we disagree with what's going on."
>
> When Indian people see us giving them the same kinds of program, they are going to call us to task on it and say, "why is a brown face giving us the same program and it is not an Indian program" . . . it's going to take a very courageous stand and it's going to take arguing with politicians, arguing with tribal councils and those kinds of courageous stands to really give the Indian people the programs they so richly deserve at this time.[55]

A similar caution is expressed by another Indian social policy analyst, Raymond Obomsawin, who writes: "What is now solely required is a culturally distinctive community development approach that will mobilize and develop local people." He continues with observations on ways of "demythologizing the system":

> It is vital that we . . . exercise a clear discernment between what constitutes the genuine and the spurious in the development. To make such a distinction is a primal step for indigenous communities who wish to effectively dismantle present debilitating dependencies, while creating a sustain-

able system.... the very doctrines and methods of modern societal institutionalization have not only established a radical monopoly over our basic physical resources and tools, but even more critically, over our education, motivation and imagination.... Indeed the system and processes of professionalist domination are so all pervasive, subtle and well rationalized that even the 'experts' actively engaged in dominating our lives, see themselves as the beneficent providers of indispensable physical or social benefits, with their roles most surely incompatible with any form of controlling exploitation.[56]

This mask of reform is disturbing. It can become a form of First Nation social control similar to what the dominant society had previously inflicted on indigenous people. While only a possibility, it needs to be considered. In a related area of the human services, the criminal justice system in Canada, this negative side of reform is referred to as the "indigenization of social control.... when indigenous people are recruited to enforce the laws of the colonial power."[57]

Possibly the greatest hindrance of ICFS reform is the foot-in-the-door it provides to erode the meaning and assurance of treaties for First Nation people.[58] The 1951 policies of the government of Canada included the phrase, "the Indian Nations will thus acquire a status identical to that enjoyed by other minority immigrant ethnic groups in Canada." An Indian lawyer, Sharon Venne, observes:

This policy ... has not changed. Canada, for the last 38 years, has tried to domesticate the treaties and terminate the indigenous people. Within the integration proposals made in the now infamous Federal White Paper, all native reserves would be eliminated, treaties terminated, federal recognition of any special status for Indians would be withdrawn, and constitutional references to "Indians and Indian lands" made a deadletter.[59]

Conclusion

This discussion began and ends with the question, "Whom do social workers serve?" In order to learn lessons about any social movement, including the specific First Nation areas considered in this chapter, one must first answer this question. Once Native and non-Native social workers are clear on their purpose, then study and action concerning "personal problems and public issues," as well as the setting of assignments to solve them, follow naturally. One cannot learn second-hand in an authentic way about change and social movement. Merely associating with those who struggle is not enough. One must "get in there and help" to realize and learn participatory alignment.

Notes

1. Bertha Capen Reynolds, "Whom Do Social Workers Serve?" *Social Work Today*, 2 (1935), p. 7.
2. Bertha Capen Reynolds, *Uncharted Journey* (New York: Citadel Press, 1963), p. 173. An invaluable source of information on the life and work of Reynolds is Joan Goldstein, "Bertha C. Reynolds – Gentle Radical" (D.S.W. thesis, Yeshiva University, 1981). For Reynolds on social movement, see *Social Work and Social Living* (New York: Citadel Press, 1951).

   There has been a rediscovery of Reynolds within the last decade, as seen in the reissue of her major writings in the National Association of Social Workers Classics Series. The formation of the Bertha Capen Reynolds Society, a national organization of progressive workers in social welfare, has been very recent. Further information is available from: Bertha Capen Reynolds Society, Columbus Circle Station, P.O. Box 20563, New York, N.Y., 10023.
3. C. Wright Mills, *The Sociological Imagination* (New York: Oxford University Press, 1959), p. 14.
4. See Fred H. Blum, "Social Conscience and Social Values," in Irving Louis Horowitz, ed., *The New Sociology: Essays in Social Science and Social Theory in Honor of C. Wright Mills* (New York: Oxford University Press, 1964), p. 169.
5. Brian Fay, *Social Theory and Political Practice* (London: George Allen and Unwin, 1975), p. 109.

6. Blum, "Social Conscience and Social Values," p. 171.
7. See Ralph Miliband, "Mills and Politics," in Horowitz, ed., *The New Sociology*, p. 86.
8. Alec G. Pemberton and Ralph E. Locke, "Knowledge, Order and Power in Social Work and Social Welfare," in Harold Throssell, ed., *Social Work: Radical Essays* (St. Lucia: University of Queensland Press, 1975), p. 37.
9. Marlene Castellano, Harvey Stalwick, and Fred Wien, "Native Social Work Education in Canada: Issues and Adaptations," *Canadian Social Work Review* (1986), p. 171.
10. James Miller, *"Democracy is in the Streets"*: *From Port Huron to the Siege of Chicago* (New York: Simon & Schuster, 1987), p. 33.
11. Paulo Freire, "Argentina: Pedagogy of the Question," *LADOC*, XVI, 6 (1986), p. 25. In his address to delegates of the World Assembly for Adult Education in Buenos Aires, Freire (p. 28) also observed: "Another virtue is to learn to experience the tense relationship between patience and impatience.... But if we break this relationship (which is just as dynamic as that between theory and practice, existence and being) in favor of impatience, we fall into an activism which forgets that history exists. In the name of a dialectical, revolutionary attitude, we fall into subjective idealism. We spend time programming, detecting a reality which exists only in the head of the revolutionary. It has nothing to do with reality. It is outside of it."
12. See Henry Giroux, *Theory and Resistance in Education* (Granby, Mass.: Bergin and Garvey, 1983), p. 242; Giroux, "Education in Democracy and Empowerment," *Tikkun*, 3, 5 (1988), pp. 30–33.
13. Moncrieff Cochran, "The Parental Empowerment Process: Building on Family Strengths," in J. Harris, ed., *Child Psychology in Action: Linking Research and Practice* (London: Croom Helm, 1985), p. 5.
14. Gisela Konopka, *Eduard C. Lindeman and Social Work Philosophy* (Minneapolis: University of Minnesota Press, 1958), pp. 142–43.
15. *Ibid.*, p. 143.
16. John Tomlinson, "The History of Aboriginal Community Work," in Rosamund Thorpe and Judy Petruchenia, *Community Work or Social Change? An Australian Perspective* (London: Routledge and Kegan Paul, 1985), pp. 161–63. Reflecting on Australian experience, Tomlinson (p. 162) observes: "At present, exactly what is likely to lead to the Aboriginal advancement is being debated all around Australia, and different Aborigines are saying quite different things. However, there are a number of points of agreement, e.g., the land rights have to be

granted, the Aboriginal health has to be taken seriously and that economic opportunities have to be made available to Aborigines."

17. See Stephen M. Rose, "Community Organizations: A Survival Strategy for Community-Based, Empowerment-Oriented Programs," *Journal of Sociology and Social Welfare*, XIII, 3 (1986), pp. 491–506. "Advocacy/empowerment" is defined by Rose (p. 494) as the necessity to understand the systemic relationship between a person's context, history, and identity – an approach to political education that supports taking issues into advocacy arenas for legal, political, or legislative action. See also Muhammad Anisur Rahman, "The Theory and Practice of Participatory Action Research," in Orlando Fals Borda, ed., *The Challenge of Social Change* (New York: Sage Publications, 1985), p. 128.

18. See Tomlinson, "History of Aboriginal Community Work," p. 162.

19. *The Years Have Spoken* (New York: privately published, 1988), p. 31.

20. Gustavo Gutierrez, *The Power of the Poor in History* (New York: Orbis Books, 1983), p. 201.

21. *Ibid.*, p. 65. For Gutierrez, this outlook of the oppressed is best described by Dietrich Bonhoeffer: "We have learned to see the great events of history of the world from beneath – from the viewpoint of the useless, the suspect, the abused, the powerless, the oppressed, the despised. In a word, from the viewpoint of the suffering."

On this same topic Gutierrez (p. 190) remarks: "Recent years in Latin America have been marked by an increased awareness of the world of the 'other' – of the poor, the oppressed, the exploited class. In a social order drawn up economically, politically, ideologically by the few for the benefit of the few, the 'others' – the exploited classes, oppressed cultures and ethnic groups that suffer discrimination – have begun to make their own voice heard. Gradually they are learning to speak without interpreters, to have their say directly, to rediscover themselves and to make the system feel their disquieting presence. They are becoming less and less an object of demagogy and manipulation, or an object of halfhearted disguised 'social work' and more and more the agents of their own history – forgers of a radically different society."

22. John Hellman, *Simone Weil: An Introduction to Her Thought* (Waterloo, Ont.: Wilfrid Laurier University Press, 1982), pp. 88, 86. Of the career of this remarkable French philosopher, theologian, and political activist who died at the age of thirty-four in 1943, Hellman (p. 88) writes: " . . . of course it was her perception of the inability of men to look at one another in this 'certain way' that was behind the

radical conclusions Simone Weil drew from her experiences as a manual labourer. Who asked the modern miner, auto worker, or fisherman, 'What are you going through?' Neither the factory bosses, nor their 'experts,' nor the trade union leaders, nor even the most perceptive revolutionaries like Trotsky seemed to ask this question. Moreover she was shocked to find that, in modern life, even workers themselves failed to ask this question of one another. Who, then, asked this question and gave true attention to the unhappy answer of the world? Her examples were, again, Charlie Chaplin and Jesus Christ."

23. Paulo Freire, *Politics of Education: Culture, Power and Liberation* (Granby, Mass.: Bergin and Garvey, 1985), pp. 127–28.

24. The Taking Control Project, a review of Indian and Native social work education in Canada funded by Health and Welfare Canada, sponsored the conference, November 8–11, 1985. See Harvey Stalwick, *What Was Said: Study Guide One* (Regina: The Taking Control Project, Social Administration Research Unit, Faculty of Social Work, University of Regina, 1986; book and videotape). See also Ann M. Scott, "First Nations and Child Welfare: Towards an Indigenous Model" (M.A. thesis, McMaster University, 1988).

25. Stalwick, *What Was Said*, p. 132.

26. Louis Lowy, *An Assessment-Survey Report of Indigenous Social Work Literature on Social Work Methodology* (Boston: Boston University, School of Social Work, 1988), pp. 46–49.

27. *Ibid.*, pp. 11, 67.

28. The Bertha Capen Reynolds Society has as its motto Reynolds's view that "It is not we, a handful of social workers against a sea of human misery. It is humanity itself building a dike and we are helping in our particularly useful way." In her biography, Reynolds expressed a similar view: "If one word is needed, then, to begin to sum up what fifty years of living have taught me, that word is *relatedness*.... It is relationships with other people that make us human and give us immortality in the heritage we leave (however small or obscure) to future generations." Reynolds, *Uncharted Journey*, p. 314.

29. Freire, *Politics of Education*, pp. 40–41.

30. Frances Fox Piven and Richard A. Cloward, *Poor People's Movements: Why They Succeed, Why They Fail* (New York: Vintage Books, 1979), p. ix.

31. Phyllis Pease Chock and June R. Wyman, *Discourse and the Social Life of Meaning* (Washington: Smithsonian Institute Press, 1986), p. 41.

32. The basic text for the dialogue-conversation between the co-authors is based on a presentation by Yvonne Howse to a Peyakowak (They Are Alone) conference held March 24–25, 1988, in Regina.

33. An excellent general reference is Julian Rappaport, Carolyn Swift, and Robert Hess, eds., "Studies in Empowerment: Steps Toward Understanding and Action," Vol. 3, Nos. 2/3 of *Prevention in Human Services* (New York: The Haworth Press, 1984). See Charles H. Kieffer, "Citizen Empowerment: A Developmental Perspective," *ibid.*, pp. 31–33; Suzanne Kindervater, *Nonformal Education as an Empowering Process* (Amherst, Mass.: University of Massachusetts, Centre for International Education, 1979).

34. Scott, "First Nations and Child Welfare," p. 103.

35. Dr. Diamond Jenness, *Plan for Liquidating Canada's Indian Problem Within 25 Years*, report to the Special Joint Committee appointed to examine and consider the Indian Act (Ottawa, 1947). The main objective of the plan was "to abolish, gradually but rapidly, the separate political and social status of the Indians (and Eskimos); to enfranchise them and merge them into the rest of the population on an equal footing" (p. 301).

36. The term "cultural genocide" is used here as defined in the Convention on Genocide, approved by the General Assembly of the United Nations, December 11, 1946, Resolution 96, Article II, section (e): Forcibly transferring children of the group to another group. See Leo Kuper, *Genocide: Its Political Use in the Twentieth Century* (New Haven: Yale University Press, 1981). In this work Kuper (p. 31) discusses the controversy on the inclusion of cultural genocide in the original draft of the U.N. Convention on Genocide and how Western European democracies representing colonial powers seemed on the defensive, sensitive to criticism of their policies in non-self-governing territories. See also Leo Kuper, *International Action Against Genocide*, Report No. 53 (London: Minority Rights Group, January, 1982). Among "ethnocidal acts" Kuper includes "the deprivations of opportunity to use a language, practice a religion, create art in customary ways, maintain basic social institutions, preserve memories and traditions, work in co-operation toward social goals" (p. 4).

37. The references to an 1874 letter by a missionary are based on conversations with J. Robb, Faculty of Law, University of Alberta, and Maria Campbell, Saskatoon, Saskatchewan.

Nicholas F. Davin, a friend of Prime Minister John A. Macdonald, was commissioned to visit and report on American industrial boarding schools for Indians. He wrote: "The Industrial School is the principle feature of the policy known as that of 'aggressive civilization'." This policy featured the transferring of children from their homes to residential boarding schools because other attempts at education failed. On this failure Davin observed, "it was found that the day school did not work, because the influence of the wigwam was stronger than the influence of the school. . . . The child . . . who goes to a day school learns little and what he learns is soon forgotten, while his tastes are fashioned at home and his inherited aversion to toil is in no way combatted." In Davin's recommendation for the establishment of industrial boarding schools, he stated: "if anything is to be done with the Indian, we must catch him very young. The children must be kept constantly within the circle of civilized conditions. . . . The plan now is to take young children, give them the care of a mother and have them constantly in hand." See N.F. Davin, "Report on Industrial Schools for Indians and Half-Breeds, to the Right Honourable the Minister of the Interior," Ottawa, 14 March 1879, pp. 1–2, 13. (Copy of printed report in Saskatchewan Archives.) See also Brian E. Titley, *A Narrow Vision: Duncan Campbell Scott and the Administration of Indian Affairs in Canada* (Vancouver: University of British Columbia Press, 1986).

38. Two of the 330 children are wards of the provincial government. The majority attend for both educational and social reasons caused largely by poverty and the underdevelopment of reserve-based support services. First Nation control is beginning to develop alternatives to residential care and the provincial child welfare system.

39. Franz Fanon, *The Wretched of the Earth* (New York: Grove Press, 1981), p. 223.

40. Videotape of a 1987 Paulo Freire workshop at the Highlander Research and Education Center, New Market, Tennessee. Available in the Highlander Library.

41. Sidney J. Fiddler, "Ethnic Competence: Social Work with Indian Minorities" (M.S.W. thesis, University of Regina, 1988), p. 137.

42. Bradford W. Morse, "Aboriginal Children and the Social Welfare State in Canada: An Overview," paper presented at the Second Conference on Provincial Welfare Policy, University of Calgary, May 1–3, 1985, p. 6.

43. Native Council of Canada, "Report of the National Day on Native Child Care: Challenges into the 1990s," Winnipeg, May 24, 1989.

44. Department of Indian Affairs and Northern Development, *1987 Indian Child and Family Services in Canada Final Report* (Ottawa, 1988), pp. 10–11.
45. Native Council of Canada, "Report."
46. Parliamentary Task Force on Program Review (Nielsen Task Force), *Improved Program Delivery: Indians and Natives* (Ottawa: Supply and Services Canada, 1986). This 523-page report was one of twenty-one volumes produced by the Nielsen Task Force.
47. Native Council of Canada, "Report."
48. *Ibid.* See also Bradford W. Morse, *Aboriginal Peoples and the Law: Indian, Métis and Inuit Rights in Canada* (Ottawa: Carleton University Press, 1989).
49. Chock and Wyman, *Discourse and the Social Life of Meaning*, p. 205.
50. Interview with Myles Horton, Highlander Research and Education Center, New Market, Tennessee, October 18, 1989.
51. Emily F. Carasco, "Canadian Native Children: Have Child Welfare Laws Broken This Circle?" *Canadian Journal of Family Law*, 5 (1986), pp. 111–38.
52. Scott, "First Nations and Child Welfare," p. 104.
53. Patricia Maguire, *Doing Participatory Research: A Feminist Approach* (Amherst, Mass.: University of Massachusetts, Center for International Education, 1987), p. 101.
54. Andrew Armitage, Frances Rick, and Brian Wharf, *Champagne/Aishihik Child Welfare Pilot Project Evaluation* (Victoria, B.C.: University of Victoria, 1988).
55. Harvey Stalwick, *Searching for My Children and Now They Are Home: Study Guide Two* (Regina: The Taking Control Project, University of Regina, 1987).
56. Raymond Ombomsawin, "Alternatives in Development and Education for Indigenous Communities in Canada," a monograph published by Indian and Northern Affairs Canada, Evaluation Directorate (July, 1986).
57. Paul L. Havemann, "The Indigenization of Social Control in Canada," in B. Morse and G. Woodman, eds., *Indigenous Law and The State* (Dordrecht, Holland: Foris Publications, 1988); Havemann, "The Over-Involvement of Indigenous People with the Criminal Justice System: Questions about Problem 'Solving,'" in Kayleen M. Hazelburst, ed., *Seminar Proceedings No. 7, Aboriginal Criminal Justice Workshop* (Canberra: Australian Institute of Criminology, 1985).
58. Havemann, "Indigenization of Social Control in Canada"; Paul L. Havemann, "Law, State and Indigenous People: Pacification by

Coercion and Consent," in T.E. Capato *et al.*, eds., *Law and Society: A Structuralist Perspective* (Toronto: Harcourt Brace Jovanovich, 1989), pp. 54–74.

59. Sharon H. Venne, "Treaty and Constitution in Canada: A View from Treaty Six," in Ward Churchill, ed., *Critical Issues in Native North America* (Copenhagen: International Work Group for Indigenous Affairs, Document No. 62, December 1988/January 1989).

CHAPTER 5

Social Work and the Labour Movement

by Ben Carniol

Introduction

In contrast to social work's roots, which grew out of the charity organizations of the late 1800s, labour unions were born in the arena of class conflict. If efforts by social workers have suggested that society could become more compassionate, the history of labour unions reflects a different approach to human well-being, namely, the development of a social movement to protect the working class from economic exploitation.

This chapter will explore the connections between social work, social change, and the labour movement. It will provide a brief overview of the labour movement. This will be followed by a focus on labour unions as potential settings for social services. I will also examine some of the implications of social work practitioners becoming unionized and active with their unions. These explorations will address how the welfare state and the system's pattern of social relations have had an impact on the labour movement and social work professionals. In that context, a progressive form of social work will be examined in terms of its practice, its constraints, and its potential.

These pages will draw on my experience as a social work practitioner and teacher, including my involvement with labour organizations as placements for over fifty students over the past four years.

The Labour Movement

Just as other social movements, such as the women's movement and the civil rights movement, have evolved in response to social injustices, so too has the labour movement. Craig Heron, in *The Canadian Labour Movement: A Short History*, notes that we have not had a single labour movement:

> Rather we have had a long series of often independent, locally or regionally based movements that rose and declined in particular periods depending on the opportunities for organizing that were created within the economy, class relations and the state.[1]

As Heron points out, unions have evolved in response to changes in our capitalist economy. The earliest organizing efforts by workers in Canada seem to have occurred during the early 1800s in pre-industrial towns. Entrepreneurs in that period were often individuals and families, usually locally based. Their workers included miners, fishermen, and construction workers. As these labourers experienced pressure from their employers to get more work out of them, sporadic protests became more organized as unions grew in the 1830s and 1840s. In those early years, the state was already hostile to labour unions, as illustrated in 1816 by the Nova Scotia legislature, which declared union organizations illegal. As well, our early courts defined union activities as conspiracies in restraint of trade.[2]

Faced with stiff opposition not only from employers but also from the state, unions in the 1800s, not surprisingly, were often short-lived and ineffective. Craft unions had their origins during this period and emphasized the workers' pride in certain crafts, such as baking, shoemaking, printing, and moulding. Many of these early craft unions were quite sexist, reflecting the patriarchal view that a woman's proper place was in the home. It has been estimated that by the end of the nineteenth century over a third of women waged workers were employed as domestic servants.[3] Other women took in laundry, accepted boarders, or did home sewing for clothing contractors, jobs that were difficult to organize because they were isolated from each other or under especially close supervision, as in the case of domestics who boarded in their employers' homes.

Nevertheless, for the many other women who did work in factories and experienced sweat shops and other exploitative conditions, their lower pay was seen as quite "natural." This attitude is expressed in a newspaper account from British Canada in 1897 reporting a clothing manufacturer's views on wages:

> I don't treat the men bad, but I even up by taking advantage of the women. I have a girl who can do as much work, and as good work as a man; she gets $5 a week. The man who is standing next to her gets $11. The girls, however, average $3.50 a week, and some are as low as two dollars.[4]

Since women's work was so devalued, men in craft unions feared that allowing women into their crafts would devalue their work and lower the wages paid to men. Therefore, these early unions tried to exclude women from "men's jobs." Despite some notable exceptions, the union movement tended to be, until recent decades, very much a male institution. From her research, Ruth Frager observes:

> For a significant number of male trade unionists, their sense of dignity – and indeed their conception of unionism – was bound up with their gender identity. The notion of the manly union member, indeed the very notion of "fraternity" and "brotherhood," defined women as outsiders.[5]

This helps to explain how such terms as "workers," "work," and "labour movement" were equated with the public arena and with waged work, to the exclusion of housework and child care traditionally done by women in the private sphere of home for no pay. Though women occasionally did take leadership roles, it was more usual for women to be excluded from decision-making in unions: "Unions commonly met in smoke-filled bar rooms, normally a masculine preserve of boozy camaraderie and sexist jokes. It is hardly mysterious that women's participation in such union meetings was so infrequent."[6]

By the early 1900s craft unions were co-existing with industrial unions, the latter responding to the emergence of large corporations and their expanding industrial assembly lines. The increased mechanization of work meant that labour became more repetitive, more controlled, less autonomous, and less skilled. As a consequence, unions covered entire industries regardless of skill or trade differences. These industrial unions were typically confronted by hostility from employers and by repression from the state. The early decades of this century saw an accelerating shift from corporate competition toward a pattern of several large firms becoming a monopoly, a pattern that in various industries had its roots in the previous century.[7] With this corporate consolidation came demands from management that workers take pay cuts in already poor wages.

Grounded in these bitter disputes, union leaders and their supporters at times looked to radical alternatives such as socialism, which influenced for instance the Wobblies (International Workers of the World) and the OBU (One Big Union) in the early 1900s. The Winnipeg General Strike in 1919 was only one illustration of the growing polarization. On the one side organized labour and the working class were pressing for the right to collective bargaining; on the opposite side, organized capital was insisting on continuing its accumulation of profits and capital. During these conflicts the state consistently took the side of capital, for example, by sending in troops and mounted police to quell peaceful demonstrations.[8]

The aftermath of repeated union defeats in Winnipeg and elsewhere resulted in a decline of union militancy, though unionists still tried to improve salaries and other terms of employment. The turning point came in the 1940s. As Heron points out:

Before that point, almost every effort by various labour movements to win a permanent place in Canadian industrial and political life was beaten back by hostile employers and a generally unsympathetic state. It was only during and immediately following World War II that unions made the breakthrough that allowed them to operate within a tightly controlled framework, in most mass-production, resource and transportation industries. That base was broadened in the 1960s and 1970s with the organization of public-sector workers.[9]

The expansion of the welfare state during and after the Second World War did not "just happen." Organized labour along with political parties on the left played a major role in pushing for medicare, old age pensions, unemployment insurance, social assistance, and social services. The labour movement has been a major force in urging governments to adopt and further develop social programs.[10]

There is a paradox here because an expanding state not only rescued capitalism from its worst excesses, such as mass poverty. It also curbed the public's dissatisfaction, provided employment, and tried to show the system cared, while at the same time consolidating the power of a primarily white, male corporate elite.[11] As the welfare state expanded, it also fuelled new demands from women, people of colour, unionists, and environmentalists, just to mention a few. A growing number of teachers, nurses, social workers, and other occupational groups within the public sector, many of them women, sought affiliation with labour organizations, thereby boosting the labour movement's membership.

The larger number of women unionists in alliance with the women's movement put pressure on unions to change. While women had at various times shown determination and resilience as strike supporters or as strikers in their own right,[12] women were no longer willing to take a back seat. As a result, as Carole Conde and Karl Beveridge note in their *First Contract: Women and the Fight to Unionize*:

Over recent years the labour movement has developed and fought legislative and bargaining campaigns for such issues as daycare, equal pay for work of equal value, mandatory affirmative action, rights and benefits for part-time workers, paid parental leave, protection from sexual harassment....[13]

A similar change, though less advanced, is also occurring within the labour movement in relation to white racism. Just as all societal structures, from the educational to the political, have been affected by institutionalized racism, unions have not been immune from it. Just as employers were able to play women off against men to drive down wages, a similar process has occurred with immigrants, especially people of colour. The devaluation of cultural and racial groups, beginning with Canada's indigenous population and extending to immigrants from Africa, Asia, the Caribbean, and Latin America, has often resulted in lower wages paid to people of colour, which has constituted a threat to the higher salaries paid to unionized and mainly white workers. Such situations have allowed management ample scope to practise its divide-and-rule tactics.

To their credit, some unions have developed human rights and anti-racism programs with the clear message that racism hurts everyone and weakens the labour movement. Such initiatives by labour have helped to revitalize this social movement into becoming more relevant to a much wider cross-section of the population, thereby strengthening labour's capacity to put upward pressure on the system, in direct conflict with the prevailing top-down power relations. In attempting to resolve these conflicts, compromises were made and were embodied in the various programs of the welfare state. Yet, these compromises were carefully constructed so as not to alter the basic structures which favoured a privileged class, gender, colour, and sexual orientation. This is illustrated by the role of the welfare state vis-à-vis the labour movement.

On the one hand, the state's laws, policies, and administration do recognize that unions and workers have certain rights. These include the rights of collective bargaining and to hold the

employer responsible for carrying out the terms of the nego-
tiated contract. Unionized employees can today use grievance
procedures to curb certain arbitrary actions by management.
Within certain unions, if their members vote in favour of a strike
after having followed the required procedures, their refusal to
work is considered a legal action, respected by our courts.

On the other hand, the labour movement may have lost more
than it gained. Leo Panitch and Donald Swartz, in *The Assault on
Trade Union Freedoms*, point out that as the state became more
interventionist, it expanded its control over unions through a
complex set of laws, policies, regulations, and tribunals to govern labour-management relations.[14] This had the effect of unions
being pushed into a pervasive technocratic/bureaucratic role,
which has meant that while unions have remained political,
they have had more difficulty practising mass mobilization.

The state's legalization of activities by organized labour had
been granted only after immense pressure from the labour
movement. But this legislation was framed in such a way to
guarantee a definitely subordinate position for labour in relation
to management. This understanding has periodically been made
explicit by Canadian policy-makers. For example, Justice Rand
of the Supreme Court of Canada pointed out in reference to the
competing claims of labour and capital: "In industry, capital
must in the long run be looked upon as occupying the dominant
position."[15] Thus, while in theory the state must ensure that no
groups exercise a disproportionate amount of power, in practice
the state favours the captains of industry.[16] Government actions
such as tax reforms and fiscal policies continue to be accompanied by promises to serve the total population fairly. Yet in
practice, the state is presiding over an increasing gap between
the richest class and the poor.[17]

As a consequence the system has disfavoured the poor – who
overlap with the unemployed, the disabled, the homeless – with
women and people of colour representing a disproportionately
high number.[18] Also disfavoured is organized labour. The state,
as largest employer, has become determined to "down-size" and
to resist higher wages for its public servants; the state has also
passed laws that threaten severe fines and jail terms for rebel-
lious unions and their leaders.

At the very time unions are under this increasing assault by the state, and when their members are increasingly laid off, fired, or disciplined because of mergers and relocations due to the increasing international flow of capital, the labour movement today finds itself severely maligned by the mass media. It seems not to matter that the overwhelming majority of unions are honest and follow democratic procedures for election of officers – unions are still stereotyped as corrupt. It matters not that most of the violence has come from police forces and from private security agents hired by management – unions are still blamed for violence. It matters not that real wages have declined since 1975 – workers are seen as greedy.[19] Neither does it matter that only 40 per cent of non-agricultural workers are unionized in Canada (in the U.S. the figure is 18 per cent) – unions are still seen as too powerful.[20] The ultimate irony is that labour is also called irresponsible, when it is that movement along with others that defends medicare and old age pensions and advocates for fairer policies in taxation, housing, daycare, social services, and other social programs.

Despite some exceptions, the media feed these negative attitudes by portraying management as constructive, labour as disruptive.[21] When there is a breakdown in labour-management relations, instead of it being named a "labour-management dispute," the label is "labour dispute," equating labour with the problem. Even the very power relations of employer-employee are portrayed in ways that distort who exercises real power. A columnist from the *Toronto Star* writes: "most union workers today have become lords of the labour market."[22] Meanwhile public-sector job losses continue: 2,800 in Montreal;[23] 12,751 teaching and non-teaching employees in British Columbia;[24] another 1,072 full-time jobs from the federal government.[25] Across the country, over 57,000 job losses have been attributed to free-trade-driven layoffs and closures.[26]

Today, as in the past, what emerges is a picture of continual struggle by waged workers, whose overall objectives can be generalized as striving for justice at the waged workplace as well as in society generally, objectives that have typically been misrepresented and undermined by employers and the state. This is not to suggest that all unionists, historically or today, want to challenge the status quo. Many do not see their role as political because they have come to accept the system's narrow definition of unions as concerned only about wages and collective agreements. Thus, not only the larger system experiences structural conflict, but the labour movement itself is permeated with these contradictions, partly due to the hegemony of attitudes that celebrate the status quo.

The Labour Movement and Social Work

Social workers are familiar with the conflicting pressures represented by management's top-down power versus empowerment from below. These contradictory pulls are also reflected by the ways that some workplaces have delivered social services to their own employees. On the one hand, management has in some cases developed human services as extensions of their personnel departments. At the same time, labour, too, has initiated its own set of social services to better meet the employees' needs. In both cases, the programs of the welfare state have been found wanting. Managers in some of the larger companies wanted to address social problems affecting their own employees. Mental stress, illness, marital breakdown, drug abuse, and other problems had resulted in employee absenteeism and loss of productivity, and, therefore, loss of profits. To reduce these losses and also to show that corporations could do more than operate on a "dog-eat-dog" basis – indeed, could have a human face – corporate managers introduced social services within their companies.

These services, sometimes called employee assistance programs or EAPS, have included the services of psychologists, psychiatrists, and social workers. For social workers who accept top-down power as "normal" and who accept corporations as benign, it follows that these management-sponsored social services will be seen as "free, on-site, available as needed and responsive to working class style and needs – frequently an oasis in a desert, without which little professional intervention on behalf of this population would occur."[27] By contrast, a very different response to EAPS is given by social workers who align themselves with subordinated groups and who are critical of the status quo. For example, Neil Tudiver of the School of Social Work at the University of Manitoba has documented that "Social services have been used in industry to motivate workers towards increased production, to placate angry employee groups, to forestall attempts at unionization, to soften the harsh effects of poor working conditions and to direct workers' loyalty to their employers' interests."[28]

EAPS have also been introduced in various public-sector organizations. Despite the growth of EAPS, however, the people who are most directly affected – the employees themselves – have indicated that, given a choice, they would prefer union-sponsored social services.[29] As a result, union counselling programs are in the initial stages of being sponsored and established by some unions, accompanied by labour-sponsored training programs to prepare unionists to respond to the personal problems of their co-workers – by listening, referring, following up, and advocating for change.[30]

Inasmuch as social work welcomes and provides support to the union counselling approach, this may result in more social services being responsive to the needs and interests of workingclass men and women. It is too early to tell whether these union services will evolve into a more extensive array of union-sponsored social services. Felicia Houtman, co-ordinator of the union counselling training program at the Metro Toronto Labour Council, cautions that "the labour movement wouldn't want to create its own social agencies if this merely becomes a stopgap measure and lets the government off the hook from its responsibilities." Much as food banks deflect attention away from the welfare state's failure to establish full employment at decent wages or to provide adequate resources to the needy, so, too, the growth of labour-sponsored social agencies could give the welfare state another excuse to further underfund social services.

On the other hand, experience suggests that when counselling is done under the auspices of a social movement, such as the women's movement and its shelters for abused women or the First Nations movement and its alternative child welfare services, the patterns of social relations change. By comparison to the hierarchical approach typical of the welfare state, these social services become oriented to the goal of equality, both within their organizational structures and within client-worker relationships. If labour-sponsored social services are similarly able to foster critical awareness and to empower staff and clients, this may generate new upward pressures on the welfare state to better respond to human need.

In terms of numbers, relatively few social workers have been involved with workplace-sponsored social services geared to their own employees, regardless of whether these have been sponsored by labour or management. Nevertheless, an indirect contribution to social work by the labour movement's counselling program has been to challenge the view prevalent among management that the major source of social problems is the individual. Labour-sponsored counselling programs are pointing to the waged workplace itself, that is, the way work is organized, the one-way flow of power – in short, the dehumanizing social relations of waged work as a primary cause of stress on individual employees.[31]

Aside from union counselling programs, there is another, more direct way in which organized labour is having an influence at least on some social workers, and that is through involvement as members of their union. Traditionally seen as women's work, social work, much like nursing and teaching, was poorly paid. With women increasingly becoming primary wage-earners, and with a new sense of independence nurtured by the women's liberation movement, social workers turned to labour unions for improved salaries and other benefits.

Today, as social agencies become more bureaucratized and as resources dwindle while unmet needs increase, social workers experience frustrations that harken back to an earlier era when social work unionism gained credibility within the profession during the 1930s and 1940s. These legacies have been noted as including not only the application of collective bargaining to improve the working conditions of social workers but also the contribution of unionism to foster a critical rethinking of social work goals and methods.[32]

At the same time, given that much of social work education and practice is so often geared to a middle-class orientation, many practitioners' views toward unions range from hostile to apathetic.[33] Lorraine Duff, unionist and social worker, formerly with the Children's Aid Society of Metro Toronto, points out:

> Most social workers don't see unions as something important. Then there's that different language. When you go to union conventions and hear people addressing each other as "brother" and "sister" – it's alien. Our agency's workers are in a small local – and our local is part of a large union which seems to be monopolized by a traditional leadership. Only now are some issues important to women, like work-sharing, beginning to be addressed by the larger union because women have been pushing for these things.

Despite these obstacles, research over the past decade suggests that the common ground between unions and social work is being rejuvenated. An American study of unionized professionals who held Master's degrees in social work found that a majority of these practitioners did not perceive a conflict between membership in a union and in a professional association.[34] This was confirmed by a Canadian study conducted by Ernie Lightman, University of Toronto, Faculty of Social Work, who asked members of a social work professional association about their perceptions of unions. He found that social workers viewed unions and professional associations as each serving different functions. Unions were seen as being most effective in the areas of wages and job security while the professional association was seen as most effective in the area of improvement of professional standards. Lightman also asked: Is it unprofessional for social workers to belong to unions? Seventy-five per cent said "no."[35]

Today at least half of the social workers in Canada belong to unions, in part because government is the largest employer of social workers and the vast majority of government employees are unionized.[36] Yet the present situation is far from static. On the one hand, corporate leaders, including the Business Council on National Issues, the Canadian Chambers of Commerce and the Canadian Manufacturers' Association, are anxious to chop back social programs.[37] By contrast, labour unions, through their conventions, rallies, and other activities, have opposed this agenda by corporate leaders. As in the past, however, the state itself is much more in alliance with business than with labour so that a neo-conservative agenda has already cut back social services, with more cuts in store. The question remains: will labour be capable of forming more effective coalitions with other movements and networks to win the public support necessary to defeat this conservative agenda?

In the meantime, unions are providing many front-line social workers with some degree of protection. As one social worker put it:

> unions are important for front line social workers because they serve as a protection against abuses by managers. By "abuses" I mean the long hours we are made to work; the heaviness of the caseload and I don't just mean numbers. Unions allow us an opportunity to have a voice, to disagree with management without getting hit with "insubordination."

Not that equality can be achieved between front-line professionals and management. Under our present system, despite unions, the welfare state and its agencies still concentrate most of the power within management. Nevertheless, social work unionists do experience a limited degree of empowerment as they press for the implementation of their rights under their collective agreements. If involvement with the labour movement can act as a brake against the disempowerment so often experienced by front-line workers, what are the implications for services to clients?

Progressive Social Work and Unions

The labour movement has generally had little direct impact on the nature of social work practice. At the same time, organized labour does represent a social movement that offers tangible evidence for more radical social workers that social change is possible. Because unions have over time come to recognize the importance of power, whether economically or politically, the mobilization of power is an important union activity. This occurs both at the union local level around collective bargaining and at the wider societal level around social, political, and economic issues. To carry this out, unions have built a permanent social action structure. Depending on the circumstances this structure can organize strikes and other job actions to bargain for better terms of employment. Similarly, this same structure organizes protests, boycotts, and other demonstrations to oppose corporate-inspired policies such as free trade or public-sector cuts.

Furthermore, the labour movement has made it possible at least for some social workers to identify themselves with disempowered classes, thereby creating an alternative from a type of elitist professionalism that aspires to prestige while defending the status quo. Inasmuch as some social workers have become either union activists or supporters of unions, these practitioners have found that the labour movement offers a welcome space to engage in radical forms of social work.

Such radicalism, to be sure, is not particularly unique to labour settings. Within the labour movement, analysis of various oppressions, such as gender, race, and class, informs progressive practice by social workers and others. Such analysis is also part of the reconstructed social work that has been articulated by feminists to include: working toward egalitarian client-worker relationships; grounding practice in the experiences and feelings of client populations; bringing together clients, workers, and others in networks, groups, co-ops, and collectives to facilitate upward power for personal and political transformation.

These elements are important features of feminist social work, pioneered by women such as Helen Levine, Canadian social work educator, who has also developed an incisive critique of conventional social work.[38] Drawing from feminist insights, Maurice Moreau of the Université de Montréal has developed an innovative structural approach to social work. When he worked with labour organizations he focused on three areas for radical practice: (a) helping with immediate resources; (b) helping with clients' feelings, ideas, and behaviours; and (c) helping with the efforts for change within social movements.[39]

The following pages will elaborate on these three areas. While labour is certainly not the only social movement to have inspired this form of radical social work, I hope to illustrate how a radical approach is being applied, at least in part by social workers active in the labour movement. What makes their practice radical is that by addressing the roots of social problems these practitioners are working toward a basic transformation of our major social structures.[40] One important site for such practice is within unionized social services.

Helping with Immediate Resources

To put it in context, radical social workers are attentive to a number of characteristics such as the social class, gender, colour, ethnicity, sexual orientation, age, and health – of themselves and of their clients. These workers tune into the combination of these qualities, and into issues of inadequate resources and the associated social relations experienced by the client.[41] From afar this area of practice may seem to be the same as conventional social work, since in both instances social workers find themselves scrounging for resources that are typically inadequate to meet the need.

Yet sharp differences also exist. Conventional social workers tend to give a certain message to clients to "adjust" or "adapt" to these insufficient resources, because these workers often feel that the system has adapted as much as it can to the clients' needs. By contrast, radical practitioners are critical of the societal structures causing insufficiency of resources and they openly share these feelings with clients. A social work unionist in a daycare setting explains:

> When I see that parents have to resign from their employment because the kind of daycare they need is not available, I always tell the parents it's not right. I refuse to defend the system which is not supporting parents. I tell parents that the daycare system is not there to respond to parents – they

expect parents to fit into their model. Some parents do fit, but many don't.

Put another way, while both conventional and progressive practitioners possess relationship skills, progressive practitioners combine these skills with the ability to link systemic power relations with the consequent lack of resources with which clients must contend. Such analysis includes an acknowledgement by workers that as professionals their class position makes them more financially secure than most clients. It includes an awareness of how workers and clients both experience different yet similar alienation, dehumanization, and insecurities stemming from the domination of male-oriented, white upper-class structures.

Radical workers recognize that sometimes the strategic use of social action can make a difference. These social workers, therefore, tend to be more motivated to use their skills and discretion in ways that at times make their advocacy for resources more effective. This also contributes to a more positive relationship with the client, who sees the worker is clearly on her side.

In addition, progressive practitioners are likely to be active with their union, which can have a direct impact on resources for clients. To illustrate, Pam Chapman refers to her experience as a front-line social worker employed by an emergency shelter:

> The shelter is an old house and meant to hold no more than 100 women and children, yet we had about 150! It was unbearable! It was summer, no ventilation – and of course, no air-conditioning. Babies were crying, mothers were yelling. There was no privacy. Stress and tension levels were way up. Can you imagine what it's like to have forty kids running loose? They're young and have energy, yet the moms are tired and depressed. This went on for eight months. We'd asked management to address worker and client concerns about this situation but they paid no heed, except to say "Yes, we're working on it." Fortunately the union did make a difference. The union steward got all the staff together and asked us to fill out question sheets, so we could list the problems and our suggestions for combatting

these problems. Besides the problems associated with the overcrowding issue, we had been pushing for a children's program in the shelter. The union then called a meeting with the shelter's management and at that meeting the union demanded action. Soon after, the children's program was established and other conditions improved as well.

This illustrates that one way for social workers to reduce the insecurity and powerlessness inherent in the employee role is to become active with their union. This is borne out by the experience of a professional who recalls her struggle to complete her social work education:

Before the union I was quite outspoken. Even so, I'd say my confidence as a worker has increased with being part of our union. Before the union I twice requested a leave of absence to finish my social work education. I was turned down twice. Two days after our collective agreement I asked again and received approval the next day!

Helping with Clients' Feelings, Ideas, and Behaviour

Practitioners know that it is easy for clients to be stripped of dignity when they belong to labelled and stigmatized groups. Typically, these negative stereotypes about welfare and unemployment insurance claimants, women, non-whites, lesbians, gay men, and other subordinated groups become psychologically internalized by those who belong to stigmatized populations. For this reason, Moreau and others point out that while workers must give primary attention to short- and long-term resource provision, it is equally important to work on "changing ideas, feelings and behaviour of clients which contribute to the client's own oppression or contribute to the oppression of others."[42]

Rather than blaming clients for "their" problems, progressive workers see clients as survivors. After being subjected to prolonged oppressive social relations, clients who are able to survive these experiences may also develop feelings, ideas, and behaviours that are destructive to themselves and to others.[43] Progressive workers help clients to explore the sources of these feelings and attitudes, drawing linkages to institutional sources.

Both conventional and critical practitioners express empathy toward their clients – but conventional practice does so in ways that focus exclusively on the individual (or the family), resulting for example in a statement by the worker: "From what you've said I can understand why you feel terrible about losing your job when the company closed down." Radical social workers also value the feelings of the individual client, but in addition they include the situation of others in similar subjugated situations. For example, the worker would say: "From what you've said I can understand why you and your co-workers feel terrible about . . . " In doing so, progressive workers apply a *social* empathy focusing on the client as well as others who may be subordinated in the same way.[44] This is similar to the process used by adult educator Paulo Freire in helping people to become aware of how others are similarly dominated and in helping them to name the wider societal institutions responsible for their oppression.[45]

The point is that it is important for social workers to address client feelings and to do so in ways that foster insight into the connections between such feelings and their sources within the workings of the dominant institutions. Put another way, using the terms of C. Wright Mills, social workers can use their counselling skills not only to provide emotional and other support to clients expressing their "private troubles," but also to help clients understand the connections between their troubles and the oppressive social relations emanating from the larger societal structures, that is, from "public issues."

The exploration into these feelings and their context is best done when professionals no longer feel they have to apologize for the status quo. Brigid Kemp, a social worker, reflects on the commonality of progressive work with clients and with her union:

> In both cases – working with clients and working with our unions – I'm discussing the politics of how the system works. We're both workers in the same system – though the client's employer is different than mine – but it's still the same system which creates the restrictions and frustrations that both of us face.

When workers analyse these frustrations in terms of the institutions that dominate the lives of *both* workers and clients, it becomes possible for workers to be more self-disclosing with their clients than is the case with non-critical workers. As social workers share more of their own tensions, frustrations, and life experiences with clients, this can develop toward a more mutual, reciprocal client-worker relationship. This is in contrast to the model where only the client does the self-disclosure and the professional does the diagnosis and treatment.

When clients recognize that the worker is on their side, it becomes easier for clients to share their own ideas and feelings so that more effective help becomes possible. That means, as a practical matter, that critical professionals act as allies with their clients and view psychological and structural change as not something for which clients alone are responsible. That such an approach can work within the agencies of the welfare state is suggested by Irwin Elman. He works with a group of youth (sixteen to twenty-one years old) who are preparing for independent living after being in foster care and group homes:

> I'm involved to a limited extent in our union and I see the larger union movement as one of the vehicles for changing the world. In the agency, we're trying to help kids change their world. So for me personally there's a connection here. It's subtle. It's a way of my withdrawing and allowing these kids as a group to take control over decisions. In the past they've been in the back seat: all decisions were made by the agency. It's scary for them to take control. They've been taught to be dependent. But now they're starting. They still seek my advice and support – but they're starting to feel it's their turn to be in the driver's seat.

As clients are helped to gain even a limited sense of autonomy, then it becomes more likely that clients and workers may raise questions about the legitimacy of existing class, gender, race, and other systemic inequalities. Such questions constitute an essential part of counselling for Lee Schore, a social worker with extensive union experience who documented her work at a California plant shut down by General Motors, when over 5,000 workers were laid off. As a result of these layoffs, the union, the company, and the state co-sponsored job retraining and counselling services. The union insisted and the company agreed that these services be provided, as Schore put it, by "professionals who could talk the workers' language."[46] Consequently the services became union-based: part of the counselling team consisted of union counsellors, that is, unionists who were known and trusted by the displaced workers and who served as natural helpers.

Schore confirmed what other studies had found – that one of the most devastating effects of unemployment is the isolation it produces. She also noted that this isolation aggravated the feelings of frustration, anger, fear, and depression so often experienced by the unemployed. Not surprisingly there were increases in family conflict and violence as well as increases in alcohol and other drug abuses. Schore summarizes the nature of the union-based counselling services that addressed the feelings and attitudes of the client population:

> Dignity was restored by helping the dislocated worker and his or her family acknowledge and legitimize their feelings of anger and fear. People were reconnected to social support networks that enabled them to overcome their isolation and utilize collective strength. This was essential in a union setting, where it was critical to retain the strength of the workers and their union. The support networks made it possible for the workers to place the blame for their situation where it belonged: on the economic system and the process of corporate decision-making, not on themselves.[47]

Helping with Social Movements

Whether focusing on helping to obtain immediate resources or on help with the clients' feelings, ideas, and behaviours, the approach here has been to include political analysis and political dialogue as an integral part of the worker-client relationship. For clients as well as workers, moving from dialogue to practical action means working politically with labour or other social movements.

The charge that social workers should leave politics to the politicians seems to assume that social work is a neutral profession. This is much like the questionable view that the state is also neutral. Curiously, professionals who are accepting of the status quo and its downward flow of power are not seen as being political. Yet when social workers support an upward flow of power they are accused, at least by some, of being "political," that is, of doing things viewed as "unprofessional."

This reveals that the very term "political" can be defined either negatively or positively depending on whether the term is used by someone who feels that existing social relations are desirable or by someone who recognizes these relations are oppressive. Since dominant power-holders will generally view the prevailing power patterns as immensely desirable, even natural, they (and their supporters) will castigate any individuals or groups, including social workers, who ally themselves with the powerless and their social movements. As Ann Withorn points out in *Serving the People: Social Services and Social Change*, "Certainly there is a bias in the current structure and practice of service delivery; our task is not to eliminate the bias but to shift it."[48]

At a practical level this means that it is important for social workers and their clients to become connected to the progressive initiatives and networks often found within social movements. One of the ways social workers in the past have connected themselves and their clients to community networks outside of their social agencies has been through the practice of community work. As a specialization within social work, a variety of community-oriented tactics and strategies have been practised and articulated in the literature.[49] Nevertheless, much like the rest of social work theory, the literature on community work has generally not addressed the over-arching structures that create and maintain systemic inequalities, such as those based on class, gender, and race. This may, however, be an example of theory lagging behind practice, because my observations in recent years suggest that many community workers are fully aware of the various oppressive institutions. As a consequence these workers are frequently active with one or more social movements, including the labour movement.

This was the case when management at the Metro Toronto Children's Aid Society announced that services to community groups would be cut. This agency's community workers, along with other social workers, were quite active with their agency's union, whose president at the time, Karen McNama, describes what happened next:

> We documented how our clientele were paying for a deterioration of our service. The biggest reason for the strike was that we had an executive director who told us there'd be no cuts in programs – then at the next board meeting there he was proposing cuts in service! This made us angry. We went out on strike and before we'd return to work we insisted that we obtain a letter from the Board stating there would be no layoffs and no cuts in services for the duration of this collective agreement. Only after we received this letter did we settle and return to work.

While this strike made a favourable difference to clients and workers,[50] is this not an exception? Are not social workers more usually blocked by the welfare state and its agencies from linking themselves and their clients with community groups and social movements? Often the answer is yes, but not always, because the control by the welfare state is not totally complete. Therefore, opportunities exist for workers and clients to coalesce into alliances of opposition to arbitrary decisions by the welfare state and its agencies. This is precisely why labour unions are so important for social workers and others.

In addition to affiliation with organized labour, empowerment from below is further advanced by workers and clients through: (1) forming client-worker support groups; (2) taking initiatives to arrange for supervisor-client-worker dialogues to tune workers and supervisors into client concerns; (3) exploring with supervisors ways of opening staff meetings to participation by clients and related social movements; (4) exploring how to institutionalize client and worker input into agency decision-making; (5) developing trust with news reporters who share a progressive perspective, so that blatantly punitive actions by management could come under the glare of publicity; (6) redefining job descriptions to allow workers to engage in progressive practice. Even where few or none of these steps are taken, it is still possible for workers to carry out progressive practice, as suggested by a social work unionist:

> The way I relate to clients challenges the relationship we are supposed to have – it challenges the social relations of that bureaucracy. Clients experience a relationship which is different from what they're accustomed to. They don't perceive you as someone they have to fight all the time, but as someone who shares the same kinds of ideas, thoughts, and interests.

It is true that resistance should be expected from management. While professional autonomy is limited by the top-down relations of the welfare state, this autonomy also exists, even if to a smaller degree, at supervisory and managerial levels. The degree will vary with the agency, but line workers should not assume that all managers want to apply top-down control. When tested, some managers have been supportive of progressive initiatives, including union activities. Clearly, labour-positive managers are the minority because those selected for promotion are usually those who have toed the management line sufficiently to attract management approval.[51] In the larger context, a labour-positive manager is a contradiction in light of the prevailing pattern of social relations. But the same can be said about social work's mandate to help within a society where power flows downward from mainly white males in the most affluent social class.

Which side of these contradictions do we align ourselves with? Just as it has been possible to establish pockets of feminist social work within a patriarchal society, or similarly, just as examples of non-racist social work have emerged despite the racist society in which we live, so, too, social service managers can choose to move against the grain. More specifically, a labour-positive manager would learn how to share major decision-making power with front-line workers and with the users of the services. At times, that would mean managers supporting the position of both front-line workers and their union in challenging certain agency decisions and policies – a process that definitely has its risks. Such oppositional work would require picking one's battles and developing allies, including support from other like-minded administrators.

Such upward power processes, whether instigated by administrators, front-line workers, clients, unions, or other movements, are partly inspired by a vision of alternative structures that could be far more satisfying than present arrangements. These alternatives come from a tradition of critical thought, which is relevant to social work and beyond it. As social work unionist Kathleen Lawrence states:

> Labour leaders must begin to convey that they understand the sources of workers' discontent by advancing demands that *cannot* be met under the present system. These demands would be widespread and varied: the re-organization of work away from hierarchical, authoritarian control toward democratizing our workplaces; the redesign of work processes away from routine, repetitive tasks; societal control over investment decisions – the socialization of profits.[52]

Aside from articulating these democratic alternatives, social movements are increasingly acknowledging the importance of solidarity among different oppressed groups. More specifically, the labour movement is strengthened when it goes to bat (as it has) for equality for women and people of colour. Indeed, the prospects for progressive change increase inasmuch as major social movements (and their supporters, including professionals) become more inclusive of each other's goals and perspectives.[53] Such coalitions are emerging and they are anchored in a concern about people, in sharp contrast to the practices of the dominant institutions. Such caring reflects values that are highly consistent with social work values.

Conclusion

Coming from a history of hostility from employers and the state, the labour movement has had an uphill struggle. In addition to being put on the defensive by dominant economic structures, trade unions had incorporated the sexism and racism prevalent in Canadian life. Only in recent years has the labour movement become more inclusive of women and people of colour. As a result, organized labour is today more congruent with its objectives, namely, to achieve justice and fair treatment both in the workplace and in society generally. Moreover, labour's ability to organize challenges to the dominant power-holders has benefited social work by holding out some hope in the feasibility of empowerment from below. There is some evidence to suggest that when organized into unions, social workers can at times put pressure on agencies and governments to benefit clients in terms of resources.

While the radical social work approach presented here is by no means confined in its practice to union activists, my conclusion is that unions offer a valuable lesson about social change. This lesson is integrally connected to labour history – a history grounded in unequal social class relations. Specifically, the labour movement today symbolizes the following message: when it comes to social change, it is insufficient to work toward the dismantling of oppressive relations in gender, colour, sexuality, ability/disability, or other areas or in any combination of these. Unless the reconstruction of social relations also includes an equal priority on dismantling the illegitimate power anchored to class privilege, the concentration of wealth into the hands of a privileged few will inevitably continue. This is the lesson incorporated into the radical social work outlined above, because it focuses attention on social class as an essential part of its approach. This position seems increasingly to reflect the approach of progressive activists inside and outside of the labour movement. Such a conclusion is also fully congruent with the application of social work values by progressive workers. As social workers and others translate these values and linkages into action, then we will be contributing to the reconstruction of our consciousness, our relationships, our politics, and our professional practice.

Notes

My appreciation goes to the following, whose excellent comments on earlier drafts of this chapter sharpened the analysis: Dorothy Moore, Pam Chapman, Maurice Moreau, Brigid Kemp, Kathleen Lawrence, Kathy Jones, Marvyn Novick, Rhona Phillips, Myer Siemiatycki, Michael Harrison, and the authors of this book. In addition, I am grateful to Patience Wilson for typing and retyping of drafts, and to Jennifer Welsh and Marvyn Novick, current and former deans of the Ryerson Faculty of Community Services, for their support of my work for this chapter. Last but not least, my thanks to the students, union organizers, and social work unionists whose ideas and comments over the years strengthened this chapter.

1. Craig Heron, *The Canadian Labour Movement: A Short History* (Toronto: Lorimer, 1989), p. xvi. For an example from the Maritimes, see Dorothy Moore, "A Social History of New Scotland," paper presented at the Conference of the British Sociological Association, University of Edinburgh, March, 1988.
2. Heron, *Canadian Labour Movement*, pp. 7, 13.
3. Ruth Frager, "No Proper Deal: Women Workers and the Canadian Labour Movement, 1870–1940," in Linda Briskin and Lynda Yanz, eds., *Union Sisters: Women in the Labour Movement* (Toronto: Women's Educational Press, 1983), p. 46.
4. *Daily Mail and Empire* (Toronto), October 9, 1897, p. 10, cited *ibid.*, p. 47.
5. Frager, "No Proper Deal," p. 56. Some exceptions included the efforts by Knights of Labour of the late 1800s to organize all workers into one large union, regardless of skill, gender, or ethnicity.
6. *Ibid.*
7. Gregory S. Kealey, "The Structure of Canadian Working-Class History," in W.J.C. Cherwinski and G.S. Kealey, eds., *Lectures in Canadian Labour and Working Class History* (St. John's: Memorial University of Newfoundland, 1985), pp. 28–31.
8. Heron, *Canadian Labour Movement*, Chapter 2.
9. *Ibid.*, p. xvii.
10. Alvin Finkel, "Origins of the Welfare State in Canada," in Leo Panitch, ed., *The Canadian State: Political Economy and Political Power* (Toronto: University of Toronto Press, 1977). See also Neil Fraser, "The Labour Movement in the Explanation of Social Service

Growth: the United States and Britain," *Administration in Social Work*, 3, 3 (Fall, 1979), pp. 301–12.

11. Nancy Adamson, Linda Briskin, and Margaret McPhail, *Feminist Organizing for Change: The Contemporary Women's Movement in Canada* (Toronto: Oxford University Press, 1988), pp. 98–99. The relationship between these forms of domination in any moment of history can be subjected to empirical study. See Michael Albert and Holly Sklar *et al.*, *Liberating Theory* (Boston: South End Press, 1986), p. 19.

12. For instance, the strike by women against Bell Telephone in 1907 and the textile strike in Hamilton in 1929. See Frager, "No Proper Deal," p. 58. Or more recently, the 1978 strike by women against Fleck Manufacturing and the 1985 "Visa strike" against the Canadian Imperial Bank of Commerce, where 80 per cent of the strikers were women. Carole Conde and Karl Beveridge, *First Contract: Women and the Fight to Unionize* (Toronto: Between the Lines, 1986), p. 72.

13. Conde and Beveridge, *First Contract*, p. 9.

14. Leo Panitch and Donald Swartz, *The Assault on Trade Union Freedoms* (Toronto: Garamond, 1988), pp. 17–27.

15. Justice I.C. Rand, *Canadian Law Reports*, 2150 (1958), pp. 1251–53, cited *ibid.*, p. 19.

16. For reference to how the courts view the contract of employment, see John Anderson and Morley Gunderson, *Union-Management Relations in Canada* (Don Mills, Ontario: Addison-Wesley, 1982), p. 65.

17. Lars Osberg, "The Distribution of Wealth and Riches," in James Curtis *et al.*, eds., *Social Inequality in Canada: Patterns, Problems, Policies* (Scarborough, Ont.: Prentice-Hall, 1988), p. 94.

18. David Ross and Richard Shillington, *Canadian Fact Book on Poverty* (Ottawa: Canadian Council on Social Development, 1989).

19. Panitch and Swartz, *Assault on Trade Union Freedoms*, p. 100.

20. *Ibid.*, p. 98.

21. Roy Adams, "Conflict and the Nature of the Industrial Relations System," *Labour Gazette* (April, 1975), pp. 220–24.

22. Frank Jones, "NDP an idea that just didn't work," *Toronto Star*, March 7, 1989, p. F1.

23. Mary Cook, chair, Ontario Division of Canadian Union of Public Employees, Job Security Committee, data presented at Ryerson Union Fair, March 9, 1989.

24. *Ibid.*

25. "Ottawa boosts its spending but cuts jobs in civil service," *Toronto Star*, April 29, 1989, p. A13.

26. Information given by Bill Howes, executive assistant, Labour Council of Metro Toronto and York Region, December 1, 1989, based on figures from *Trade Watch*, Canadian Labour Council, October, 1989.

27. Bradley Googins and Joline Godfrey, *Occupational Social Work* (Englewood Cliffs, N.J.: Prentice-Hall, 1987), p. 5.

28. Neil Tudiver, "Forestalling the Welfare State: The Establishment of Programmes of Corporate Welfare," in Allan Moscovitch and Jim Albert, eds., *The "Benevolent" State: The Growth of Welfare in Canada* (Toronto: Garamond Press, 1987), p. 186.

29. Paul Newman, "Program Evaluation as a Reflection of Program Goals," in Ray Thomlison, ed., *Perspectives on Industrial Social Work Practice* (Ottawa: Family Service Association Canada, 1983), p. 107. See also Graham Lowe and Herbert Northcott, *Under Pressure: A Study of Job Stress* (Toronto: Garamond, 1986), pp. 109-19.

30. Gail Lem, "Helping hand may work best at arm's length" and "Program's primary purpose is to assist the worker," *Globe and Mail*, January 3, 1987, Section B, pp. 1, 3.

31. Lee Schore, *Occupational Stress: A Union-Based Approach* (Oakland, California: The Institute for Labour and Mental Health, 1984).

32. Leslie Alexander, "Unions: Social Work," *Encyclopedia of Social Work*, 18th edition, vol. 2 (Silver Spring, Md.: National Association of Social Workers, 1987), pp. 794-95.

33. Dena Fisher, "Problems for Social Work in a Strike Situation: Professional, Ethical and Value Considerations," *Social Work*, 32, 3 (May-June, 1987), p. 253. For a description of resistance to unions by directors of voluntary social agencies, see Milton Tambor, "Unions and voluntary agencies," *Social Work*, 18, 4 (July, 1973), pp. 41-47.

34. Leslie Alexander, Philip Lichtenberg, and Dennis Brunn, "Social Workers in Unions: A Survey," *Social Work*, 25, 3 (May, 1980), pp. 216-23.

35. Ernie Lightman, "Professionalization, Bureaucratization and Unionization in Social Work," *Social Service Review*, 56, 1 (March, 1982), p. 137. See also Susan Braungart, "Social Workers out for New Standards" and "Social Workers plan Strike Vote," *Calgary Herald*, April 1 and March 31, 1989. This information sent to me by Yvonne Schmitz, social worker and activist with Local 6 of the Alberta Union of Public Employees.

36. Joan Pennell, "Union Participation of Canadian and American Social Workers: Contrasts and Forecasts," *Social Service Review*, 61, 1 (March, 1987), pp. 123, 130, and note 56. Pennell estimates that the percentage of social workers in unions by the mid-1970s had

reached 50 per cent in Canada (and climbing) while it was only 15 to 20 per cent in the U.S. (and also climbing).

37. "Corporate Canada seeks cuts in social spending," *NAPO News* (Ottawa: National Anti-Poverty Organization), No. 24 (Winter, 1989), p. 2.

38. Feminism has proven to be a fertile source for such reconstruction. For instance, see Helen Levine, "Personal Is Political: Feminism and the Helping Professions," in Angela Miles and Geraldine Finn, eds., *Feminism in Canada: From Pressure to Politics* (Montreal: Black Rose, 1982); Ketayun Gould, "Life Model versus Conflict Model: A Feminist Perspective," *Social Work*, 32, 4 (July-August, 1987), pp. 346-51. For an early attempt to link social work and client empowerment via unions, see Milton Tambor, "The Social Worker as Worker: A Union Perspective," *Administration in Social Work*, 3, 3 (Fall, 1979).

39. Maurice Moreau, "Structural Social Work Practice: A Case Illustration," Montreal, 1985, available from l'Ecole de service social, Université de Montréal. See also by M. Moreau, "A Structural Approach to Social Work," *Canadian Journal of Social Work Education*, 5, 1 (1979), pp. 78-94; M. Moreau in collaboration with Lynne Leonard, *Empowerment Through a Structural Approach to Social Work: A Report from Practice* (Montreal and Ottawa: Ecole de service social, Université de Montréal, and Carleton University, School of Social Work, 1989).

40. Ben Carniol, "Clash of Ideologies in Social Work Education," *Canadian Social Work Review, 1984*, p. 192.

41. Moreau, "Structural Social Work Practice," pp. 1-4.

42. *Ibid.*, p. 4.

43. Levine, "Personal Is Political," p. 192. Levine examines how the helping professions have contributed to self-destruction by women.

44. Social empathy is referred to by Maurice Moreau in his "Practice Implications of a Structural Approach to Social Work," *Journal of Progressive Human Services*, 1 (forthcoming, 1990).

45. Paulo Freire, *Pedagogy of the Oppressed* (New York: Herder & Herder, 1971).

46. This information was sent to me by Lee Schore, "The Fremont Experience: A Counselling Program for Dislocated Workers," *International Journal of Mental Health*, 13, 12 (1984), p. 161.

47. *Ibid.*, p. 168.

48. Ann Withorn, *Serving The People: Social Services and Social Change* (New York: Columbia University Press, 1984), p. 213.

49. For instance, Brian Wharf, ed., *Community Work in Canada* (Toronto: McClelland and Stewart, 1979); Ben Carniol, "Democracy and Com-

munity Development in Canada," *Community Development Journal* (Oxford), 18, 3 (1983), pp. 247–50; Bill Lee, *The Pragmatics of Community Organization* (Mississauga, Ont.: Common Act Press, 1986).

50. For further documentation on this strike, see Lois Sweet, "Strikers say kids' welfare is at stake," *Toronto Star*, June 23, 1986, p. C1.
51. This point was made by Dorothy Moore in reviewing a previous draft of this chapter.
52. Kathleen Lawrence, "Deepening Workers' Demands," paper for Labour Education, Ontario Institute for Studies in Education, 1986, p. 17.
53. Ben Carniol, "Social Work and Social Change: Breaking Out," in Carniol, *Case Critical: Challenging Social Welfare in Canada*, Second Edition (Toronto: Between the Lines, 1990). See also Dennis Howlett, "Social Movement Coalitions - New Possibilities for Social Change," *Canadian Dimension*, 23, 8 (November-December, 1989), pp. 41-47.

CHAPTER 6

Lessons from the Social Movements

by Brian Wharf

The task of this concluding chapter is to determine if lessons can be learned from the three social movements that will aid the profession of social work in pursuing or rediscovering an agenda of social reform. Before launching into this discussion, it is important to note that all of the case studies confirm the basic position presented in Chapter 1 that the state acts in the interests of the rich and powerful. The progressive achievement of the state in establishing rights to education and health care and to a limited number of income security programs is welcomed and applauded. However, the failure of the state to establish rights to income and housing, to recognize women's work in caring for children and the aged as valued and recompensable labour, and to redistribute income in a more equitable fashion is regretted and criticized. The Canadian state is viewed as an uncertain welfare state, one reluctant to establish policies that would promote the equality of women, Natives, and workers.

This context is important because it places the efforts of social movements in proper perspective. These changes are viewed as illegitimate by those possessing power and influence in Canadian society since they are aimed at redistributing wealth and power. They are therefore fundamentally different from changes sought in the days of the settlement house movement. Changes then were directed at the eradication of obvious evils, such as child labour practices, and were often supported by representatives of all classes, including the upper class.

For social work the struggle is complicated by the fact that the profession is now a prisoner of its own reforms. Social workers are largely employed by state departments, which are large, hierarchical organizations providing inadequate benefits and services. These organizations are controlled by politicians and policy-makers who cherish the status quo. In fact, as Joan Gilroy points out in Chapter 3, social workers have become part of the problem rather than advocates for social reform:

> Social work is deeply enmeshed in the structures of inequality that exist in the wider world, including the inequality between women and men. The dominant models of theory and practice are inherently sexist and oppressive to women. In addition, social workers' location in government or government-funded agencies makes their participation in the struggle for women's equality very problematic.

In Chapter 4, Yvonne Howse and Harvey Stalwick have identified social workers as oppressors – as representatives of a white society that has oppressed Native people. Indeed, their indictment is shared by many Indian leaders and social workers, who now view "the sixties scoop" (a decade in which well-meaning but misguided white social workers apprehended Indian children) as cultural genocide.[1] Howse and Stalwick repeat the message that not only has the profession of social work been largely unconnected to the First Nation movement, but in the not so recent past social workers have been part of the problem rather than part of the solution.

With regard to the labour movement, Ben Carniol in Chapter 5 notes that since "much of social work education and practice is so often geared to a middle-class orientation, many practitioners' views toward unions range from hostile to apathetic." However, Carniol points out that "the common ground between unions and social work is being rejuvenated." As the examination of connections between social work and social movements continues in this chapter, a potential for collaboration does emerge.

The remainder of the chapter is organized in the following fashion. The lessons from the case studies are presented first. Building on this discussion, some specific suggestions are made for change in social work education and practice and in the auspices through which social services are presented. A third section is devoted to developing a middle-range strategy for change focused on the community. The chapter concludes with a discussion of the potential of social work to contribute toward changing the fundamental structures and institutions in Canadian society. Hence, the chapter directs attention to change at the level of the individual, community, and society.

Lessons from the Case Studies

While the case studies did not yield a set of specific strategies waiting to be picked up by social work, there is a rich lode of experience and insights in the accounts of these social movements that could benefit social work in pursuing social reform. The intent here is to identify and describe these insights using the Moreau framework introduced by Carniol in Chapter 5. This framework consists of three components: helping clients with immediate resources, helping with client feelings, and linking to social movements.

Helping with Immediate Resources

As the case studies make clear, social workers are well aware that the social programs they administer are often inadequate to meet the needs of their clients. Like other human service professionals who work in poorly supported health and legal aid programs, social workers become inured to these inadequacies and in turn expect their clients to adjust and make do. Needed is a transforming ideology to enable social workers to overcome the pressure to accept inadequate benefits. The case studies suggest that incorporating the ideology of a social movement is one way of achieving this transformation. Thus, Carniol states that "radical practitioners are critical of the societal structures causing insufficiency of resources and they openly share these feelings with clients." Carniol goes on to argue that unions provide a source of protection for workers who decide it is not sufficient simply to share feelings but that they must take action on behalf of clients. Carniol provides several examples of union-based advocacy actions that have been effective.

In the same vein, Gilroy notes that "transition houses for battered women, rape crisis centres, feminist counselling, and health services were all established under the auspices of the women's movement." These local services have effectively met the needs of many women despite struggles for funding from United Ways and various levels of government. And certainly in some communities feminist social workers have been conspicuous leaders in developing these resources. Similarly, Howse and Stalwick describe the emergence of Indian Child and Family Services in a number of provinces. The involvement of social workers in these programs and in the Taking Control Project of the Faculty of Social Welfare at the University of Regina provide examples of social work's support for First Nation control.

Helping with Client Feelings: The Concept of Social Empathy

A crucial aspect of the kind of social work practice advocated by the authors of the case studies is the concept of social empathy identified by Carniol. By social empathy Carniol means not only avoiding the all-too-common practice of blaming the victim but providing information about the reasons for unemployment, poverty, poor housing, and violence to women. In effect, social workers become educators. As Carniol states, "social workers can use their counselling skills not only to provide emotional and other support to clients expressing their 'private troubles,' but also to help clients understand the connections between their troubles and . . . 'public issues.' "

With respect to violence against women, the concept of social empathy requires an understanding of the structural aspects of Canadian society where men have more power than women, and where violence in many forms is condoned. Feminist counselling, as Gilroy explains, adopts an educational focus in enabling women to "see that problems such as physical abuse, which had been considered individual and unique, were in fact common and widespread, and were rooted in women's social and political subordination." An instructive example of responding appropriately to client feelings is contained in one case reported by Gilroy in Chapter 3. In this instance the student not only accepted the client's definition of her situation but fought against the attempt of the agency to reframe the situation as a personal trouble.

In the case of child welfare among First Nation peoples, social workers can assist by acknowledging with aboriginal clients the mistakes made in generations of child-care practice vis-à-vis aboriginal families and children. Howse and Stalwick argue:

> Support for this [social reform] to happen will come from social workers who come to realize that much of past and present social work practice with Native families is bad practice – with the best of intent it has destroyed families. Dialogue is one way of empowering people to name their oppressors, to expose conditions and take this necessary first step in freeing all people, social workers included, to connect personal troubles with social issues.

Linking to Social Movements

The case studies suggest that the reform agenda of social work could be strengthened by forging three specific connections between social work and social movements. The first link is between individual social workers and social movements. Gilroy makes the point that becoming a feminist social worker heightens the frustration of social work practice, and on a day-to-day basis this is undoubtedly so. Yet, identification with a social movement allows one to embrace and be sustained by an ideology. None of the social movements discussed here has achieved its objectives and none believes it will do so in the near future. What sustains social movements through the bleak days is faith in a vision of a more just and humane society. Social workers have their bleak days, and working with the labour, women's, or First Nation movements may sustain social workers in variety of ways.

The same can be said in regard to clients. If any groups in Canadian society have bleak days, they are the poor, the women, and the aboriginal clients of social welfare agencies. All of the case studies emphasize the empowering effect of belonging to and participating in social movements. Such movements emphasize that an individual is not alone in experiencing powerlessness, violence, and poverty. Further, by joining with others of similar experience and being united by a determination to alter power structures and enhance opportunities, the oppressed can create changes, even if slowly. Gilroy expresses the point eloquently:

> How can we as social workers overcome the barriers to developing feminist consciousness? How does working collectively help to bring about personal and social changes?
>
> By collective is meant co-operative work among people who develop a shared vision of a world of humanity and justice for all, the goal of remaking social institutions to respond to human needs and to foster equality, and the task of creating ourselves as new people, loving, nurturing, peaceful, and capable of living in community with each other. Collective work, then, is rooted in shared experience and consciousness. Feminist consciousness is born from the experience of being female in a patriarchal society, of living as a woman in a world that treats women as inferior, as incapable of making adult decisions, and as objects of all types of abuse. Women live in very different conditions, but most have experienced sexism in some form. Awareness of the personal effects of oppression is the basis for consciousness and collective work. *Empowerment* is the explicit purpose of collective work. Through working together with some degree of shared experience and consciousness, people empower themselves to change their lives and the world.

The concept of empowerment is discussed more extensively in a later section of this chapter.

The second link is for social workers to provide leadership in developing appropriate programs. Mention has already been made of the contribution of feminist social workers who have participated in the development of transition houses, rape relief centres, and other services that not only meet the needs of women but are governed and operated in keeping with feminist principles. Similarly, Carniol notes the potential for union-sponsored social service programs which are responsive to the needs of workers and managed in a participatory rather than an authoritarian style.

Howse and Stalwick note that social work and social move-ments have some common values:

> Social workers must . . . acknowledge that while most Indian families are oppressed and poor, they have the power within to affect the direction of their lives. It seems to us that this is the reality that must be described because – to follow an old social work dictum of beginning where the client is – only as this reality is recognized and dealt with will there be any prospect for change.

Howse and Stalwick go on to argue that social work practice and child-care programs should be built on Native values and tradi-tions, and that social workers should take part in this enterprise. Clearly, then, while social workers have not been closely asso-ciated with social movements in the past, the case studies do suggest some common grounds and point to some beginning connections.

Some readers might take the position that the connections between social movements and social work posited here go too far in suggesting ways in which social workers can contribute to social change. Such readers would agree with Paulo Freire, who has said:

> This then is the great humanistic and historical task of the oppressed: to liberate themselves and their oppressors as well. The oppressors who oppress, exploit and rape by virtue of their power cannot find in this power the strength to liberate either the oppressed or themselves. Only the

power that springs from the weakness of the oppressed will be sufficiently strong to free both.[2]

The prophetic power of Freire's position has been expressed in the sudden and spontaneous uprisings by the people against oppressive regimes in the Soviet Union, East Germany, Czechoslovakia, and Romania. However, it may be that Freire's position is not so applicable to Western democracies, where the same savage conditions of oppression do not exist. Oppression in the West is more subtle, and partnerships among labour, business, and government, as have occurred in Scandinavian countries, are possible.

The above discussion aside it will be recalled that social work students are the primary target audience for this book. Too often, critiques of the social work profession have been so devastating that they have left students with an overwhelming sense of despair. Are there no opportunities to contribute to social change? Should I simply give up any hope of working for social change and concentrate energies on becoming a skilled therapist? Unwittingly, then, the critics may have done too well. Books such as *The Politics of Social Services*, *Social Work Practice*, and *Case Critical*[3] may cause students to abandon social change in favour of careers as therapists.

The following suggestions for reforming social work practice, changing the auspices through which social services are provided, and contributing to large-scale structural change are, admittedly, middle-of-the-road pragmatic suggestions. They will be dismissed by some as fanciful and impractical and by others as insignificant tinkerings with an unsatisfactory welfare state. A principal reason for advancing these suggestions is to stir up debate among social work students and practitioners. Indeed, the six contributors to this book began the task of writing with the assumption that they shared the same ideologies but ended with the recognition that some significant differences in outlook exist. All agree with the position that Canadian society is largely controlled by an elite group of men who exercise their power to protect and enhance their own interests, and that the consequence of this exercise of power is that women, workers, and members of First Nations are oppressed and poor. However, we disagree about what to do. With the exception of the discussion on social work education, the remainder of the chapter represents the views of the editor and not those of the authors of the case studies.

Changing Social Work Education

Chapter 2 describes the experiences of the Carleton School of Social Work in its struggle to develop a curriculum that would embrace personal and social change within a dialectical and evolving perspective. Roland Lecomte points out that the accommodation achieved to date "is a mix of critical theory (Marxist theories and radical humanism) and feminist theories." He emphasizes that the search for an integrated framework of personal and social change continues within the school.

Nevertheless, the achievements of the Carleton School are considerable. The calendar clearly indicates the commitment of the school to examine "the structural context of personal and social problems" and it defines structural context as "the inter-action between personal, social, political, and economic aspects of such problems." In addition, and most importantly, it states: "The program focuses on the development of forms of practice . . . seeking . . . to change the nature of the interaction between people and their structural context." Analysis of class, gender, and race are considered central to the Carleton program.

However, Carleton is one of a small number of schools in Canada to have made a specific commitment to address social change in the curriculum. Most Canadian schools have avoided such a commitment and in so doing reflect the dominant ideology in Canadian society that individuals are more powerful than social conditions in creating programs. As the case studies and the discussion to follow indicate, the contributors to this book do not share this ideology; rather, we advocate following the example of Carleton and some Australian schools of social work, which have made an explicit commitment to "confronting disadvantage within a context of social justice."[4]

The first change suggested here is that schools of social work examine the respective contributions of personal and social forces to problems and on the basis of this examination declare a commitment. It is clear that the contributors favour the precedent established by Carleton in declaring a commitment to social change. In turn, a commitment to social change means that the ecological framework currently dominating the theory base of social work practice be replaced by more appropriate theoretical frameworks. As Gilroy suggests, "social welfare policy and services are not informed by an analysis of women's inequality and exploitation in the private sphere of home and family and in public spheres such as employment." Women continue to be viewed as wives, mothers, and homemakers rather than in their equally valuable and often necessary roles as workers.

Gilroy claims that feminist analyses of social policy and social work practice have not yet been included in the mainstream of social work. Her view is reinforced by other feminist writers. Pascal, for example, states, "Feminist analysis is most obviously about putting women in where they have been left out, about helping women on the stage rather than relegating them to the wings."[5] At first glance the omission from social work of a feminist view is striking since the majority of social workers and clients are women. But seen from a feminist perspective, the omission is understandable. Social work is women's work: caring for children, the handicapped, and the elderly is a job for women and women are still primarily viewed as wives, mothers, and caregivers. The omission accurately reflects the fact that men have power and women do not.

While still on the margin of theory and practice in social work, feminist analysis not only has revealed the oppressed state of women but has pointed to their crucial importance as professionals, caregivers, and consumers. Once revealed, these insights ring true. They correspond to practice experience in social work: women are, in fact, the oppressed clients of the social welfare system and women's contribution in raising children and caring for other dependents is inadequately recognized and compensated by a society that nevertheless relies heavily on such caring for its continuance. To take but one example, a single mother with children and without an income derived from employment receives a social allowance that condemns her and her children to live beneath the poverty line. Should this existence result in neglect, the children might be apprehended and placed in a foster home. A foster mother would then receive a much larger but still inadequate sum of money. Caring for children – whether in daycare, in foster care, or at home – is devalued work despite the fact that it is essential work.

Feminist analysis does not appear antagonistic to the ecological perspective. Analyses of individuals in their environments can surely include an examination of who enjoys advantage and who confronts disadvantage in these environments. However, on closer examination the two perspectives are not compatible because they are based on fundamentally different assumptions about society, how it works, and how changes are achieved. As noted in Chapter 1, the ecological perspective assumes that "all forms of life strive towards a goodness of fit with their environment."[6] Some proponents of the ecological approach, such as James Garbarino, have explicitly acknowledged the impact of poverty and poor housing. Garbarino writes that "one need not be a Marxist to recognize that the principal threat to family life is impoverishment, and that economic inadequacy, a social rather than simply a financial concept, jeopardizes the parent-child relationship."[7] But despite the contributions of Garbarino and others, the ecological perspective has not focused attention on social issues and conditions. Rather, by largely ignoring power the ecological perspective all too easily allows us to concentrate on changing the behaviour of individuals and families.

The most trenchant criticism of the ecological approach has come from feminist social workers. Thus Gould argues that "being a woman in a sexist society introduces such a potent intervening variable that any assumption of confluence between individual and societal good is an unwarranted conclusion." Gould goes on to claim that a conflict model is most congruent with a feminist perspective. The conflict model recognizes the disparities in the distribution of power and income in society and, rather than insisting that all individuals have an equal chance of attaining power and wealth, argues for changes in the policies and structures that create the imbalance: "A key concept in the analysis of social change is alienation, not defined as separation from the dominant group but as separation from a desired state of affairs. Social problems therefore reflect the failure of society to meet changing individual needs."[8]

The above discussion has emphasized the contribution of feminist theory in pointing to the inadequacies of the ecological framework. And given that the majority of social workers and the clients served by social agencies are women, feminist theory should occupy a central place in a revised social work curriculum. However, feminist theory might well be combined with the analyses of race and class in Canada. Certainly these analyses are congruent and would lead to similar conclusions regarding the position of the ethnic minorities, the poor, and women in Canada.

This would lead quite naturally to the second suggested change – the study of power in Canadian society. The issue of power is a recurring if not always explicit theme in the case studies, and a convincing case can be made that social work students should be as familiar with the phenomenon of power and how it works as they are with human growth and behaviour. The study of power can inform practice by analysing its distribution in all relationships and groups. Such examinations typically reveal that those who hold power usually favour the status quo. More importantly, the views and preferences of the powerful determine if change will occur and the direction of change. This generalization holds at all system levels, from marriage to national social policy. For the authors of the case studies such analyses are crucial. Gilroy explains: "Relationships between and among people will remain central, but these will be understood in the context of the wider world in which they take place – the world of grossly unequal power between women and men, poor and rich, black and white . . . . "

A third required change is to revise courses on social work practice and the planning of change. At the present time such courses emphasize an orderly, rational process of problem-solving guided by an expert in the planned change process. Rarely do they address the "irrational" aspects of planned change – the contributions of owed favours, personal relationships, the sudden availability of resources, among other factors. Change at all levels usually proceeds in a "muddling through" fashion whereby small changes occur in an incremental, sometimes planned, but often accidental or fortuitous fashion.[9] Nor do such courses typically explore in sufficient detail varying interpretations of rationality. For example, the values and priorities of politicians are based on their determination to stay in power and be re-elected. Plans based on such values often conflict with those built on analyses of economic and social needs. Bruce Doern captures the point nicely:

> Far more often than is warranted, the politician, as he approaches political policy-making, is viewed as being fuzzy, unsystematic, and ad hoc. With respect to the exercise of setting goals and choosing among alternative goals, the charge of being unsystematic may be very true. If, however, as I often suspect, the charge is based on little or no appreciation of the problems of securing social acceptance and compliance, then it needs to be said that the politician is not unsystematic, but rather is dealing with a different system of behaviour and political values.[10]

Thus the recent decision in British Columbia to establish a University of the North in Prince George has been criticized as irrational by many in the post-secondary educational system – in fact, not only irrational but a complete waste of money. But the decision takes on a decidedly different hue when viewed from the perspective of the Social Credit government anxious to shore up its fading political future and from the perspective of citizens in Prince George and other northern communities. For these citizens, southern B.C. has been favoured too long and it is eminently rational to transform post-secondary education in B.C.

A final suggestion for revising social work curricula is to include an examination of social movements in Canadian society. The three social movements examined in this book are of particular relevance to social work since low-income workers, women, and First Nation residents form the bulk of the clientele served by social workers. While the study of social movements would at one time have been severely limited by the lack of scholarly works, such is not the case today. A rich literature exists on the women's and labour movements and one is beginning to emerge for the First Nations.

The ecological perspective has made an important contribution to social work. Nevertheless, it neglects power and its distribution in society and hence does not take into account how the structures of society are responsible for creating conditions of advantage for some people and conditions of disadvantage for others. People who live in advantageous situations are labelled as successful and hard-working, whereas disadvantaged people are seen as incompetent or just plain lazy. In fact, individuals play an important but not all-encompassing role in creating the conditions in which they live. This understanding is crucial in order to appreciate how public issues of poverty and homelessness are created and sustained.

It is not the intent here to develop a blueprint for a new social work curriculum. Rather, as noted at the beginning of this discussion, it is our view that schools of social work should grapple with the personal/social change dilemma and on the basis of this examination develop both a philosophical position and a curriculum to meet this perspective. It is, however, our hope that some schools will declare a commitment to the disadvantaged and will anchor their curricula around the study of class, gender, and race, giving particular attention to the subject of power and its distribution in Canada. From these anchorpoints flow some suggestions for changing social work practice.

Changing Social Work Practice

The notion that women, Natives, and workers should be empowered to have more control over their day-to-day lives and their destiny shines through all of the case studies. Indeed, empowerment is a popular and much examined concept in social work. Despite its popularity the concept lacks precision. The following discussion attempts to remedy this deficiency.

Rappaport views empowerment as a process.

> It is the means by which people, organizations and communities gain mastery over their lives. Empowerment implies that new competencies are required in a context of living life rather than being told what to do by experts. It means fostering local solutions by a policy which strengthens rather than weakens the mediating structures between individuals and the larger society: neighbourhoods, families, churches, clubs and voluntary associations.[11]

Chris Brown has provided one of the more comprehensive discussions of the empowerment concept. He identifies six aspects or action dimensions of empowerment.[12]

1. *Affirmation of the worth and dignity of individuals.*

2. *Legitimizing and accepting the client's definition of her situation,* and of her right to prescribe a plan of action.

3. *Encouraging togetherness through sharing experiences* between clients and promoting the development of mutual aid and self-help groups and voluntary associations.

4. *Control over resources.* "The hard question, perhaps the hardest faced in social work practice, is whether in the absence of material resources one contributes anything of use to the process of empowering people."[13]

5. *Opening space for control.* Brown notes that clients typically lack control over institutions that serve them, and reminds us of the empowering effect of agencies like the Brotherhood of St. Lawrence in Melbourne:

> The Family Centre Project, therefore, attempted to break down the formal, false and often authoritarian relationship between professional staff and poor families. It encouraged the fullest participation of members in every aspect of the Project, both in specific relationships between individuals

and in the overall management and decision-making within the Project.[14]

6. An interactional component that calls for *going beyond professional and objective analysis and intervention*. This component calls for social workers to be human, to share their personal experiences, and to reach out to clients with heart as well as mind.

These action dimensions represent core values in social work and their importance in empowering clients is illustrated by again referring to Chapter 3 and the example of the woman who required temporary care for her children. Rather than accepting the client and her right to self-determination, the agency response was to redefine her situation. And it is in fact difficult for social workers to accept client definitions if these constitute an indictment against the employing agency. Nevertheless, as this example shows, social workers can change the customary response, can provide appropriate assistance and achieve a successful outcome.

A flagrant violation of the concept of self-determination has occurred in Native communities. As Yvonne Howse and Harvey Stalwick document, child welfare workers have not accepted the Native client's definition of her situation and have ignored the community context surrounding the problem of child neglect and abuse. Such culturally inappropriate practice has resulted in Native children being taken from their homes and placed in white foster homes outside Native communities. This response has proved to be both offensive and ineffective and is now being changed by First Nation ownership of child welfare.

A final comment on the importance of accepting the clients' definitions is needed and it is based on the contributions from the feminist literature. The traditional view of the family is of a haven – a safe place to retreat from the troubles of the world and the workplace. The writing of feminists such as Helen Levine[15] and insights gained from practice have forced social workers to realize that for many women the home is not a haven but rather a prison, sometimes a prison characterized by brutality. A policy response based on this analysis comes from the work of probation officers in B.C., who argued that the usual response of mediation and reconciliation counselling was inappropriate and just plain wrong in family situations characterized by wife abuse. Rather, the appropriate response is for a criminal complaint to be laid against the husband. Only after that charge has been dealt with should family court staff offer mediation services. This argument was accepted by senior staff in the Corrections Branch and became branch policy.[16]

Brown's enumeration of the dimensions of empowerment combines the traditional social work values of self-determination and respecting the dignity of the clients with more recent insights derived from knowledge of the benefits of participation. While bringing some precision to the concept, Brown's discussion leaves unanswered the intriguing question of whether one group of relatively powerless people can assist in empowering another group.

Here the key word is "relatively." As emphasized throughout this book, social workers do not have the power to change social policies at the national, provincial, or even agency level. Indeed, line staff members are often frustrated by their inability to change even minor regulations in order to increase the quality of their work life. Nevertheless, it is clear from practice and documented in research studies that at the point that policy affects clients it is the line worker who determines whether policy will be rigid or flexible. Thus Michael Lipsky's study of street-level bureaucrats (social workers, legal aid officers, public health nurses, and police officers) documents the case that "street level bureaucrats primarily determine how policy is implemented, not their superiors."[17] From the client's perspective the social worker decides whether a child will be apprehended, and the probation officer decides whether the pre-sentence report will recommend probation or jail. To clients, social workers have power, and social workers can begin the empowering process by sharing their power. This is the essence of the concept – the willingness to share the power one has with those who have even less power. Sharing power involves providing clear and accurate information about relevant legislation and agency policy; it involves allowing and encouraging clients to perform tasks themselves; and it involves them in deciding on the course of action to be taken. Carniol provides several illustrations in his chapter of social workers who empowered clients by providing information and in so doing assisted clients to recognize that they were not responsible for unemployment nor for inadequate provision for daycare.

The vision of social work practice espoused in this book is congruent with that advanced by Jordan. Jordan identifies six characteristics of this preferred approach to social work practice.

(i) We have to develop skills of negotiation. We have to explain, discuss, take account of clients' points of view, adapt our methods to their needs. We have to be influenced by individual clients, groups and communities. We have to shape ourselves to their expectations and aspirations, not simply impose our own.

(ii) Hence we have to be adaptable and flexible in our methods, to use a number of different approaches, to present alternatives, and preferably to offer clients choices.

(iii) We have to be able to work in a wide variety of conditions, including chaotic and disorderly situations. We have to be effective within very formal situations (such as courts) and in very informal, rowdy, conflictful, or bizarre situations.

(iv) We have to be more open minded about what's best for clients, what they need, and what we can offer them. We have to consult them more about outcomes.

(v) We have to know about how society as a whole works, rather than a specialized sector of behaviour or interaction. We have to understand how families, communities and neighbourhoods function, how other agencies work, how power is exercised and resisted.

(vi) We have to understand the whole context in which our clients' lives are led – the social, economic and political context, as well as the psychological, legal and medical.[18]

Nonetheless, neither the Brown nor the Jordan conceptualization goes far enough since both fail to align social work explicitly with clients and with the oppressed. The position taken here is that there should be no doubt whose side the profession is on:

indeed, the code of ethics of the Canadian Association of Social Workers states:

> Social work is a profession, committed to the goal of effecting social change on society and the ways in which individuals develop for the benefit of both.
>
> Social workers are accountable to the people they serve, to their profession, and to society, and the well being of persons served is their primary professional obligation.[19]

Changing Agency Auspices

The personal social services, and the auspices through which these services are provided, need to be considered. The term "personal social services" has been developed to describe counselling, support, and information services for individuals and families, as well as services that seek to develop the capacity of groups and communities.

Income security programs are excluded from the definition, though this should not be construed to infer that income security programs are unimportant. They are of fundamental importance, but although traditionally considered as a social service these programs are more appropriately aligned with employment. Individuals receive income from government when jobs are not available or when they are too sick, too young or too old, or occupied with other responsibilities such as child care and thus are unable to earn an income through employment. Receiving a substitute form of income should not therefore be considered an issue that requires the intervention or the professional assistance of a social worker. It is, or rather should be, an issue requiring little or no judgement, but rather a relatively automatic right to which those who cannot work are entitled.

The argument for changing agency auspices is that it is time for provincial governments to get out of the business of providing social services. This position has been enunciated and largely adopted by Ontario, Quebec, and Winnipeg and is favoured by a number of writers. For example, in the examination of the Community Resources Board experience in B.C. the writer and his colleagues recommended that provinces should have responsibility for four major functions: the determination of policy and priorities; overall financial planning and the allocation of budgets; establishing and monitoring standards of care; and the operation of specialized services.[20]

The recommendation that provincial ministries relinquish responsibility for providing direct services is based on the argument that these ministries are extremely large, with detailed policies and procedures to govern the day-to-day activities of their staff. To ensure that these regulations are carried out, organizations require supervisors and inspectors. As regulations multiply and the supervision intensifies, the capacity of the workers to exercise discretion, to own their jobs, and to feel a sense of obligation and responsibility diminishes. In the end, these organizations become characterized by rigidity and centralized control and provide inhospitable work environments for social workers and other human service professionals. These developments have been chronicled by a number of writers, including Lipsky, Carniol, and Fabricant. In "The Industrialization of Social Work Practice," Michael Fabricant concludes:

> Workers are no longer able to consider problems holistically; instead they are fit into a production process that fragments both the problem and the potential contribution of social workers. Clearly the craft elements of social work are being shattered by the increasingly rigid and mechanistic practices of large public sector service agencies.[21]

The industrialization of social work practice has resulted in social workers becoming mere functionaries carrying out rules and regulations in a mechanistic fashion. Organizing work in this way means that social workers have little or no power and are unable to respond to clients in a flexible fashion. They spend much of their time attempting to explain why benefits are inadequate and why program guidelines are rigid and unyielding. Auspices and work environments that empower social workers and their clients clearly are needed.

To be sure, the model whereby provincial ministries delegate the responsibility for direct services while retaining the policy, standard setting, and budgeting portfolio creates stresses and strains. In particular, the model runs counter to the principle that spending should be tied to the tax base, and it means that provincial officials are constantly beset by requests from local authorities for additional funds. Nevertheless, out of this scrum of competing interests some intelligent decision-making can emerge. Provincial officials develop a perspective based on needs, resources, and experiences in all parts of the province, and this perspective is a useful lens through which to evaluate the particular priorities of local communities. The interplay of provincial and community perspectives has much to commend it since the interests of the province as a whole are balanced against community needs.

The partnership between province and community for developing policy for the social services would be enhanced by adopting the example of the Social Welfare Commission in New Zealand. The Commission of eight includes Maori and women representatives and is responsible for social welfare policy. Provincial social policy commissions, to ensure that the rights of clients and minority groups are represented in policy debates, would be a marked improvement over the existing closed structures.

The argument that the public sector should delegate responsibility for providing services has been questioned by many observers of the social service scene. Among others, Hurl claims that services provided in Ontario by non-government agencies "have been judged to be of questionable standard, poorly managed, non-innovative, non-responsive, bureaucratic, poorly located, inappropriately used and non-representative of clients and community."[22] Hurl argues further that delegation obscures accountability (who is responsible when services are of poor quality – the funder or the provider or both?) and that it creates an unduly complicated service delivery system. In turn, fragmented service systems create demands for the co-ordination and integration of services and to date few satisfactory strategies for resolving the problems of co-ordination have been found.

However, many of the above criticisms can be levelled at service systems governed and managed directly by provincial governments. Thus Armitage notes that "There are some excellent services in B.C. but the system as a whole is flawed by gaps, inadequate resources, a lack of accountability . . . and a devastatingly low level of morale."[23] His observations are buttressed by the results of a stakeholder's survey of the Ministry of Social Services and Housing undertaken in March, 1988.[24]

Are you kept adequately informed by the ministry?	No – 65%
Is SS&H's service delivery effective?	No – 71%
Are the services equitable?	No – 65%
Can they be improved?	Yes – 94%

Analysis of the Quebec experience in reforming social and health services supports the line of argument being developed here. As a consequence of the Castonguay-Nepveu Commission Report of 1966, Quebec established a uniform pattern of publicly supported health and social services in the province. In a very real way these reforms brought Quebec out of a medieval era dominated by the church and contained the promise of providing universal access to services through decentralized and locally controlled centres. However, while local integrated health and social services centres were established, the control of benefits, programs, and staffing levels was retained at the provincial level. And the consequence of decentralization of services without delegation of authority and responsibility has led to the following conclusion by Shragge and Lesemann: "Large scale centralized services although providing benefits on a universal scale through rational planning lead to powerlessness and alienation of those who provide and receive benefits."[25]

The point to be established is that the nature of the delivery system (state-run or delegated) does not determine effectiveness. Rather, the crucial ingredient is the commitment to reduce inequities, eliminate poverty, and provide funding for the social services. This commitment has been conspicuously lacking in all provinces and on the part of the federal government. Hurl's criticism of Ontario is equally applicable to other provinces.

Cautious that they upset the economic balance the more economically liberal societies of which Ontario is an example have kept welfare allowances at a basic minimum, public housing at insignificant levels and social services on a residual model assisting only after the family is at risk. One must question if, with the neglect of these factors, social service systems can be established which truly address issues of equity and justice, and which attend to even the most basic needs of children and families.[26]

Given this lack of commitment, an important question is: which of the two models, state-operated or delegated authority, can develop a partnership between professionals and citizens and enhance the power base of the social services? The currently favoured privatization model whereby governments award contracts to a large number of small agencies and individuals clearly does not possess this potential, and it is not the model of choice here. Neither is the provincial ministry model, since it excludes participation by all except civil servants and elected members of the legislature. The model of choice is one where representatives of the community or the constituency served govern, and the rationale for this position is based on arguments contained in the case studies. While stopping short of constructing a model for social service in aboriginal communities, Howse and Stalwick clearly favour aboriginal control. Similarly, Carniol makes the point that union-controlled services are preferred by workers, and Gilroy clearly favours having services for women controlled by women.

At first glance the proposal for community or constituency control sounds far-fetched. Would it simply repeat the current privatization model? Would it create duplication and confusion on the inter-agency scene? Who would decide which constituency should govern which service? Which constituency, community, race, sex, or others should be given priority? Would such arrangements enhance or detract from accountability and efficiency?

However, sorting out these questions might not be as difficult as first imagined. Certainly only band and tribal councils would be awarded ownership of services for First Nations and, similarly, only union auspices would be appropriate for providing services to their members. The major difficulty would arise vis-à-vis services for children and families, including child protection, family support, and prevention programs. In geographic areas with definable boundaries and a distinct sense of community the mandate to provide family and child development services could be awarded to a community-based organization. In areas lacking these characteristics a women's co-operative or transition house might become the family and child development centre. The suggestion that such organizations might take on the responsibilities of a family and child development centre is new, but not without logic or historical precedent. The logic of the case, of course, is that women are and always have been the primary caregivers in the home, in foster homes, and in settings such as daycare and family support places. Why not, then, extend the principle and create comprehensive agencies governed by women, staffed by women, to serve women and children. Such centres could combine a wide range of programs dedicated to the support and well-being of families. Additional support for the argument comes from a recent review of the settlement house movement. As contrasted to male leaders of settlement houses, Trolander observes that "women leaders had a special sensitivity towards the problems of poor women and children. . . . What the women brought to the Settlement movement was an outraged sense that something should be done to help the poor. They were influential in changing national attitudes."[27]

An example of the kind of reframing of practice that can be expected from family and child development centres governed by women comes from the Barnardo Waverley Centre in New South Wales, Australia:

This agency – Barnardo's Waverley Centre – has purposefully set out to alter the relationships between the women involved by changing both their roles and their perceptions of foster care. The agency has replaced competition between women for the "ownership" of children with the concept of shared parenting, in which more experienced women are helping less experienced women in their capacity as paid workers. With the emphasis switched to tasks carried out for payment, the natural mother's perception of the foster mother changes from seeing her as a rival – a better mother – to viewing her as a paid service provider, from whom she can expect skilled service. This new role places the foster mother in a similar position to other paid caretakers in the community, such as teachers, day care mothers, and residential care workers. In turn, foster mothers perceive natural mothers to be important people whose wishes are to be honoured. Under this system, the foster mother can identify with the problems of the natural mother, and her job satisfaction is related to the rapid return of the child to his or her natural family, when possible, because restoration of the child is the sign of a job well done.[28]

The centre has changed the distribution of power between those who provide and those who receive services. Altering the balance of power is a very effective strategy for empowering clients and, as this example indicates, one that can be put into place by social workers and community-controlled agencies.

The establishment of agencies governed by communities and constituencies would mean that services were owned by people committed to them and, hence, who cared deeply about issues of effectiveness and accountability. We know from such disparate sources as *In Search of Excellence* and Bregha's study of the benefits of participation in the human services that when people identify with and are committed to an organization they work hard to achieve the desired results.[29] Additional evidence comes from the First Nation tribal councils that govern child welfare services. Councils view these services as being of fundamental importance because they represent the commitment of First Nation people to caring for their children. To date, evaluations reveal native-owned programs are effective.[30]

A Middle-Range Strategy: From Personal Troubles to Community Concern

A case example of the kind of social work practice that has changed the focus of practice from the individual level to the community is the Champagne/Aishihik Child Welfare Project in the Yukon initiated in May, 1986. The project sought to demonstrate that child welfare services could be managed by the band council, and this delegation of responsibility was achieved by an order-in-council of the Yukon territorial government.[31] In May, 1988, an evaluation of the project was carried out by a three-person team from the Faculty of Human and Social Development from the University of Victoria. The evaluation concluded that the project had been successful. While eighteen children had been placed away from home because of neglect and abuse, all of these placements were sanctioned by parents, and all children were placed in the homes of relatives and friends. Thirteen children had been returned to parental homes at the time the evaluation was conducted. The delegation of responsibility for child welfare to the Champagne/Aishihik Band was made permanent in 1989.

The Champagne/Aishihik project illustrates practice informed by knowledge of the environment and by the values and tradition of the people themselves. The approach to practice developed in the C/A project is best described as family-centred and community-based. Its primary characteristics include the following.

1. Child welfare has been reframed from a paramount concern with the protection of children to a recognition of the family as the first resource for the nurture and protection of children. This reframing also requires that families be held responsible for the care of children. This is a continuing and essential responsibility that cannot be avoided or evaded.

2. Given the primacy of family care, any form of substitute care is by definition secondary and temporary. Where family care breaks down the first response is to provide support in the form of counselling or very temporary respite care by relatives or friends. If these responses are inadequate, a placement in a Native child-care home may be required. Thus in this project it is recognized that a number of short and temporary care arrangements may be necessary and that a pattern of care from parents to relatives to child-care homes and back to parents is preferable to long-term substitute care.

3. The assistance of family and relatives is sought when parents experience severe problems. Family meetings are held to

plan for the care of the children and to resolve the difficulties facing parents. In turn, this planned involvement of family members and perhaps of elders and friends transforms the private matter of child welfare into a community concern.

4. The development of community-based resources both to support families currently experiencing difficulty and to prevent such difficulties is an integral part of practice. Thus, in Haines Junction and in Whitehorse, the social worker has developed Indian child-care homes to serve Champagne/Aishihik children.

The Champagne/Aishihik project provides an example of reframing individual problems into community concerns. Inability to care for one's children may be precipitated by alcohol or the breakdown of a marriage, but the response of the Champagne/Aishihik band is to arrange care in the community, to view this as a temporary arrangement, and to work toward reunification of the family. The Champagne/Aishihik approach to practice reminds one of the settlement house worker who in her dual role as a community resident and a social worker was able to orchestrate the resources of the community in a caring fashion. A significant achievement of the Champagne/Aishihik project has been to transform the private matter of child welfare into a community concern; this represents a tangible example of a reframed approach to practice with community/constituency control.

To this point the Champagne/Aishihik community has not tackled the public issues that contribute to child neglect and abuse. The secure economy of the band, with its road and house construction and other enterprises, means that poverty and unemployment are not as significant problems as in many northern communities. Nevertheless, there are serious public issues yet to be confronted by the band, including the lack of opportunities for employment and education.

The Champagne/Aishihik project immediately raises the question as to replication. Can it or similar versions be repeated in other communities? Is it possible to replicate only in other Native or very small and closed communities? A number of precedents can be cited to demonstrate that a family-centred and community-based approach to child welfare is feasible. Further, there is some beginning evidence to support the argument that such an approach can reduce the number of children removed from their families and placed on a permanent basis in foster or adoptive homes. Communities as different as Regent Park in Toronto and Indian bands in Vanderhoof, B.C., Enderby B.C., and the Dakota Ojibway Tribal Council in Manitoba have established family and child services based on a community development model that involves residents in providing programs and creating new resources in the community. These projects have supported families and empowered residents to take charge of their lives.[32]

The argument developed thus far is that it is desirable and feasible to pursue a middle-range strategy of dealing with personal troubles within a community context. Such a context allows social workers and social agencies to include within their mandate the need to change local environments as well as to deal with personal troubles. It allows social work to pursue the development of agency structures controlled by communities or constituencies and characterized by workplace democracy. It does not allow social work to confront public issues, as defined by Mills.

Social Work and Structural Change

The discussion thus far has argued that the profession of social work can push for several changes that would empower both the profession and the clients it serves. To review quickly, the profession can:

- in concert with the social movements of labour, women, and First Nations, work toward constituency and community control in order to provide appropriate services and to create a system of governance and style of practice that empowers both workers and clients;
- make an explicit commitment to promote the cause of the disadvantaged – there can and should be no doubt whose side social work is on: it is committed to the cause of

social justice and an even distribution of power and benefits in society;

• reform social work education so that social workers become experts in understanding the concept of power and its distribution in Canadian society in communities and in families; in addition, courses on the planning of change must emphasize that change rarely occurs in an orderly fashion but usually in a disjointed and incremental fashion;[33]

• work in concert with these movements to bring about social change to develop services appropriate to the needs of workers, women, and First Nation citizens.

An eloquent statement of the kind of partnership that could be achieved by social workers and social movements is expressed in the following segment of a poem written by a member of the Dakota Ojibway Tribal Council:

Just as only Indian people
can devise the strategies
to survive oppression,
it is only people with influence
and credibility
in white Canada and circles of
power who can devise the
strategies to detoxify the
structures of Canada
from the poison of oppression
and the disease of suppression.

You are the ones
who can define the strategies
to help Canadians come to grips
with institutionalized oppression[34]

An additional point not covered in the above discussion relates to the information possessed by social workers and social agencies about individual and social conditions. To the present time the stock of information has been largely restricted to the conditions of individuals. Thus, records of the number of people receiving social assistance or the number of abused and neglected children are counted and presented in annual reports of ministries and agencies. If these numbers rise they provide ammunition for developing more stringent regulations governing eligibility for service or for acquiring additional staff. But the information has not been collected from a perspective of individual-family-community and society, nor does it seek to capture the connections between these levels. Given a connective rather than restrictive lens the information could become an inventory of social conditions as well as an aggregated total of individual conditions. Social workers could become social reporters: what does my caseload tell us about the connections between poverty, homelessness, and other social conditions and private troubles in this community? Such information would supplement that compiled by Statistics Canada and other data-gathering agencies by its insistence on making connections and its emphasis on the impact of social conditions. Statistics Canada figures on poverty have become anonymous and lack any sense of urgency and pain. They resemble reports of starving populations in Abyssinia – a reported condition with which we can barely identify. The profession of social work could contribute to social change through the social reporting function. The information could provide a solid basis for all activist groups, including social movements and the profession of social work, to use in campaigns for change.

The changes discussed thus far are restricted to altering conditions at the community level. They do not address the fundamental issue of power and its distribution in society. A number of writers in social work have made this point effectively. Eric Shragge points to the dilemma in the following terms:

> Building alternative neighbourhood-controlled social and health services is the direction to go if we want to move beyond the present trends of centralization and domination. Building alternative institutions implies taking back power and control into neighbourhoods and daily life. . . . However, building alternatives is not adequate by itself. Isolated

173

social and health service projects although perhaps providing less alienating services cannot progress beyond that unless they are linked in a federated network with other similar projects and social movements.[35]

The problem, of course, is how to build these federated networks or, more bluntly put, to challenge the power elite. It is instructive to recall the Mills definition: "A public issue is a public matter: some value cherished by the public is felt to be threatened."[36] While Canadians are concerned about the extent of poverty, particularly among the elderly and among children, while we are often annoyed by reports of high salaries and the excessive perks enjoyed by the leaders of industry, and while we are frustrated by our inability to develop a more responsive system of government that would distribute power and income more equitably, we still cling to a value system that cherishes rugged individualism and extols the myth that Canada is an open society in which anyone can succeed with the requisite amount of hard work and determination. As Gilroy notes in Chapter 3:

Conventional social work often includes the assumption that individuals are more powerful than social conditions in creating problems. In this respect, it reflects the dominant belief system, the dominant ideology, of the larger society. Human beings are seen as unique, as members of a particular family, as self-determining, and as experiencing private troubles requiring confidential professional treatment. Factors such as gender, race, social class, and age are not explicitly viewed as systemic determinants of opportunities for jobs, education, health, and material resources. People are assumed to interact with one another and with social institutions on an individual, free, and relatively equal basis. Social welfare policy and programs, developed by neutral (if not benevolent) governments, are understood to express wide agreement on values and human needs. As a consequence of these beliefs, the foundation of professional social work is considered to be the knowledge and skills required to work with individuals and families on what are seen as personal problems.

Given the position taken in this book that a power elite effectively runs the country and that the cherished values of that elite call for the maintenance of the status quo, the likelihood of achieving structural changes at the societal level is dim indeed. Does this gloomy prospect mean that we should confine ourselves to individual and community change? If not, how are we to proceed?

Perhaps a start can be made by identifying some cherished values that are threatened by the existing arrangements. Children are a cherished value. Social work knows a good deal about children and how their abuse and neglect are shaped by poverty and inadequate environments. However, we have largely responded to child abuse and neglect by attempting to change the behaviour of individuals. When these efforts fail, we seek to protect children by providing substitute care. Thus, this problem is seen as being confined to individuals: provide effective treatment for parents or, in the case of severe abuse, punish the parent and the problem will be solved – until it recurs or the next complaint is heard. Our assessment and our response to this problem have mirrored, not informed, societal opinion.

The point is that we have not developed a contextual response, nor have we sought to educate the public about the context. Despite the plethora of literature arguing for an ecological approach, we continue to deal with child neglect as a private trouble. But it is both a private trouble and a public issue, and it is a "value cherished by the public [that] is felt to be threatened."

An additional argument for pursuing this strategy is that child welfare has been assigned to social work. To be sure, the state has allotted insufficient resources to this assignment, and social work has been content to respond to child abuse in a manner that does not challenge the conventional view. But an empowering approach to practice provided through agencies controlled by communities or constituencies might well enable the profession to transform child welfare. If child welfare can be viewed within a context of family, community, and society, social work might then be able to argue for strategies of change that cover all levels and do not simply allocate blame and responsibility to the individual and the family.

The work of the Child Poverty Action Group and the Coalition of National Child and Family Agencies demonstrates that some social agencies and activist groups have identified poverty as a major Canadian social problem. Further, these organizations show the strong connections between poverty and child abuse and have proposed strategies to end child poverty.[37]

The above represents only a beginning. Some readers will contend that it is an unsatisfactory and inadequate beginning because it does not constitute a sufficient denunciation of capitalism and the power elite, nor does it suggest powerful strategies for overthrowing this system. Others will argue that only the oppressed can bring about widespread changes in our social structure. Still others will maintain that only as social movements become involved in the political process of governing Canada will there be any likelihood of change. While agreeing with the argument that inequality is rooted in the capitalist free enterprise economy and with the need to alter this structure fundamentally, we need to acknowledge that the task of constructing an explicit statement of a new society is daunting, and to date this has defied the imagination of social movements. Lacking such a statement, we are largely limited to social reforms rather than fundamental social change.

It is desirable to suggest visions of a new order without being compelled to identify the specifics of such a vision. Without the spur of continuing demand for transforming society, no changes will occur. And certainly one ally for social work can be the social movements discussed here. Gilroy concludes her chapter with the statement that "If social workers make common cause with the feminist revolution in our time, then we can struggle together toward the freedom, justice, peace, and community for which we all long." Social workers should also make common cause with the aboriginal and the labour movements in struggling for a more just and humane society. Indeed, joining in the work of these movements affords a very appropriate strategy for individual social workers.

To conclude, it will be recalled that the primary objective of the book was to determine if social work could profit from the experience of social movements in addressing public issues. Two points deserve particular mention.

First, while social work and the women's, First Nation, and labour movements share a common mission of striving for a society in which power and resources are distributed in a more equal fashion than obtains at the present time, this common mission has not resulted in clear and close connections between the profession and these social movements. The case studies suggest that social movements are grounded in power theory, seek fundamental changes in Canadian society, and are prepared when appropriate to engage in conflict strategies. By contrast, social work education has neglected the study of power and its distribution in families, communities, and society, and social work practice has focused its attention on private troubles rather than public issues.

Second, it is clear that social work is not a social movement. It is a profession and its efforts toward change are constrained by several factors, such as agency auspices and provincial policies. Nevertheless, the question remains: can social work shift its agenda to include more attention to public issues? The final chapter has suggested that a thorough examination of power, class, race, and gender should be included as integral components of social work education. Given a complete understanding of the situation facing their clients, social workers could develop and implement approaches to practice that empower women, Natives, and workers. Several examples of empowering approaches are contained in the case studies. Social workers can also push for the establishment of policies and agency auspices that support empowering forms of practice. These reforms will not fundamentally alter basic social and political structures in Canada but they are compatible with and support the efforts for social change made by social movements. Such reforms will, in the words of Bertha Reynolds and Chief Angus McLean, ensure that social workers "get in there and help."[38]

Notes

1. See, for example, Patrick Johnston, *Native Children and the Child Welfare System* (Toronto: James Lorimer, 1983), p. 23.
2. Paulo Freire, *Pedagogy of the Oppressed* (New York: Continuum Publishing, 1985), p. 28.
3. Jeffry Galper, *The Politics of Social Services* (Englewood Cliffs, N.J.: Prentice-Hall, 1975); Galper, *Social Work Practice* (Englewood Cliffs, N.J.: Prentice-Hall, 1980); Ben Carniol, *Case Critical: The Dilemma of Social Work in Canada* (Toronto: Between the Lines, 1987).
4. Allan Halladay, "Confronting Disadvantage Within the Framework of Social Justice," in Edna Chamberlain, ed., *Change and Continuity in Australian Social Work* (Melbourne: Longman Cheshire, 1988), p. 59.
5. Gillian Pascal, *Social Policy: A Feminist Analysis* (London: Tavistock, 1980), p. 1.
6. Carel Germain and Alex Gitterman, *The Life Model of Social Work Practice* (New York: Columbia University Press, 1980), p. 302.
7. James Garbarino, "An Ecological Approach to Child Maltreatment," in Leroy Pelton, ed., *The Social Context of Child Neglect and Abuse* (New York: Human Sciences Press, 1981), p. 231.
8. Ketayun Gould, "Life Model Versus Conflict Model: A Feminist Perspective," *Social Work*, 32, 4 (1987), p. 348.
9. See Charles Lindblom, *The Policy Making Process* (Englewood Cliffs, N.J.: Prentice-Hall, 1968).
10. Bruce Doern, *Political Policy Making* (Montreal: The Private Planning Association, 1972), p. 11.
11. Julian Rappaport, "Studies in Empowerment: Introduction to the Issue," *Prevention in Human Services*, 3, 2/3 (November, 1984), pp. 3–4.
12. Chris Brown, "Social Work Education as Empowerment," in Chamberlain, ed., *Change and Continuity in Australian Social Work*.
13. *Ibid.*
14. Connie Benn, *The Developmental Approach: Demonstration Projects in the Brotherhood of St. Lawrence* (Sydney: University of New South Wales Social Welfare Research Centre, 1981). See also Michael Liffman, *Power for the Poor* (Sydney: George Allen & Unwin, 1978).
15. See Helen Levine, "The Personal Is Political," in Angela Miles and

Geraldine Finn, eds., *Feminism in Canada* (Montreal: Black Rose Books, 1982).

16. Brian Wharf, *From Initiation to Implementation: The Role of Line Staff in the Policy Making Process* (Victoria, B.C.: University of Victoria School of Social Work, 1984).

17. Michael Lipsky, *Street Level Bureaucracy* (New York: Russell Sage Foundation, 1980).

18. Bill Jordan, *The Identity of Social Work*, Occasional Paper No. 85 (St. Lucia: University of Queensland Department of Social Work, 1985), p. 4.

19. Canadian Association of Social Workers, "Code of Ethics" (Ottawa, 1983).

20. Michael Clague, Robert Dill, Roop Seebaran, and Brian Wharf, *Reforming Human Services: The Experience of the Community Resource Boards in B.C.* (Vancouver: University of British Columbia Press, 1986).

21. Michael Fabricant, "The Industrialization of Social Work Practice," *Social Work*, 30, 5 (1985), p. 393. See also Lipsky, *Street Level Bureaucracy*; Carniol, *Case Critical*.

22. Lorna Hurl, "Privatized Social Service Systems: Lessons from Ontario Children's Services," *Canadian Public Policy*, 10, 4 (1984), p. 397.

23. Andrew Armitage, *The Future of Family & Children's Services in B.C.: An Agenda for Reform and Research* (Victoria, B.C.: University of Victoria School of Social Work, 1989), p. 22.

24. *Ibid.*, p. 103.

25. Eric Shragge, "Foreword," in Frédéric Lesemann, *Services and Circuses: Community and the Welfare State* (Montreal: Black Rose Books, 1984), pp. 18–19.

26. Hurl, "Privatized Social Service Systems," p. 403.

27. Judith Trolander, *Professionalism and Social Change* (New York: Columbia University Press, 1987).

28. Brenda Smith and Tina Smith, "For Love and Money: Women as Foster Mothers," *Affilia*, 5, 1 (1990).

29. See Thomas J. Peters and Robert H. Waterman, Jr., *In Search of Excellence* (New York: Warner Books, 1982); Francis Bregha, *Public Participation in Planning, Policy and Program* (Toronto: Ministry of Community and Social Services, n.d.).

30. Andrew Armitage, Frances Ricks, and Brian Wharf, *Champagne/ Aishihik Child Welfare Pilot Project Evaluation* (Victoria, B.C.: University of Victoria, 1988); Peter Hudson and Brad MacKenzie, *Evaluation*

of the Dakota Ojibway Child & Family Services, prepared for the Dakota Ojibway Child and Family Services and the Evaluation Branch, Department of Indian Affairs and Northern Development.

31. It should be noted that the example of the Champagne/Aishihik band is used here because it represents an example of a model of service where community and constituency control were combined. In developing this model the band worked directly with the Yukon territorial government since no treaties exist in the Yukon. Band councils in the provinces have taken the position that provincial governments have no jurisdiction and that an agreement must be reached between a band council, representing an aboriginal nation, and the federal government, representing another nation.

32. See, respectively, Douglas Barr, "The Regent Park Community Services Unit: Partnership Can Work," in Brian Wharf, ed., *Community Work in Canada* (Toronto: McClelland and Stewart, 1979); Brian Wharf, "Toward a Leadership Role in Human Services: The Case for Rural Communities," *The Social Worker*, 53, 1 (1985), pp. 14–20; Jack MacDonald, "The Child Welfare Programme of the Spallumcheen Indian Band in B.C.," in Ken Levitt and Brian Wharf, eds., *The Challenge of Child Welfare* (Vancouver: University of British Columbia Press, 1985); Hudson and MacKenzie, *Evaluation*.

33. See Lindblom, *The Policy Making Process*.

34. Cited in Barbara Cameron, "Barriers to Success of Holistic Health," *Canadian Review of Social Policy*, No. 25 (May, 1990), p. 75.

35. Shragge, "Foreword," pp. 22–23.

36. C. Wright Mills, *The Sociological Imagination* (New York: Oxford University Press, 1959), p. 8.

37. *A Choice of Futures: Canada's Commitment to its Children* (Ottawa: Canadian Child Welfare Association, 1989).

38. See Chapter 4, notes 25 and 28.

Contributors

Ben Carniol   holds degrees in social work and law (M.S.W., McGill and L.L.B., Toronto) and is a professor at the Ryerson School of Social Work in Toronto. He has centred his social work career on client advocacy and social change organizations. His recent book, *Case Critical*, examines social work practice in Canada.

Joan Gilroy   is an associate professor at the Maritime School of Social Work, Dalhousie University in Halifax. She holds a B.A. from Dalhousie, an M.S.W. from the Maritime School of Social Work, and an M.A. (Criminology) from the University of Toronto. Her scholarly interests focus on feminism and social work, particularly on constructing feminist approaches to practice.

Yvonne Howse   is a social development educator with the Indian Student Education Centre, Prince Albert, Saskatchewan. She has been a Plains Cree/Blood advocate for alternate forms of child and family care for over twenty years in several provinces and was involved as researcher with the Taking Control Project of the Faculty of Social Work at the University of Regina.

Roland Lecomte   is an associate professor and was until recently the Director of the School of Social Work, Carleton University, Ottawa. His scholarly work has been focused on social work education and radical approaches to social work practice. His advanced degrees are from Ottawa University (M.S.W.) and Bryn Mawr (Ph.D.).

Harvey Stalwick was the founding Dean of the Faculty of Social Welfare at the University of Regina. Dr. Stalwick holds an M.S.W. from UBC and a Ph.D. from the London School of Economics. He co-ordinated the Taking Control Project and has continued to support the reform of programs related to Native people, including social work education.

Brian Wharf was the founding Director of the School of Social Work and until recently the Dean of the Faculty of Human and Social Development at the University of Victoria. His recent scholarly work has been in the child welfare field and the most recent publications include *The Challenge of Child Welfare* (with Ken Levitt) and *Toward First Nation Control of Child Welfare*.

Bibliography

Abramovitz, Mimi. "Making Gender a Variable in Social Work Teaching," *Journal of Teaching in Social Work*, 1, 1 (Spring/Summer, 1987): 29–52.

Adams, Roy. "Conflict and the Nature of the Industrial Relations System," *Labour Gazette* (April, 1975): 220–24.

Adamson, Nancy, Linda Briskin, and Margaret McPhail. *Feminist Organizing for Change: The Contemporary Women's Movement in Canada*. Toronto: Oxford University Press, 1988.

Albert, Michael, and Holly Sklar *et al*. *Liberating Theory*. Boston: South End Press, 1986.

Alexander, Leslie. "Unions: Social Work," *Encyclopedia of Social Work*. 18th edition. Vol. 2. Silver Spring, Md.: National Association of Social Workers, 1987.

Alexander, Leslie, Philip Lichtenberg, and Dennis Brunn. "Social Workers in Unions: A Survey," *Social Work*, 25, 3 (May, 1980): 216–23.

Anderson, John, and Morley Gunderson. *Union-Management Relations in Canada*. Don Mills, Ont.: Addison-Wesley, 1982.

Armitage, Andrew. *The Future of Family & Children's Services in B.C.: An Agenda for Reform and Research*. Victoria, B.C.: University of Victoria, School of Social Work, 1989.

Armitage, Andrew, Frances Rick, and Brian Wharf. *Champagne/Aishihik Child Welfare Pilot Project Evaluation*. Victoria, B.C.: University of Victoria, 1988.

Austin, David. "The Flexner Myth and the History of Social Work," *Social Service Review*, 57 (September, 1983): 357–77.

Avis, Judith Myers. "Deepening Awareness: A Private Guide to Feminism and Family Therapy," *Journal of Psychotherapy and the Family*, 3, 4 (Winter, 1987): 15-46.

Bailey, Roy, and Mike Brake, eds. *Radical Social Work*. London: E. Arnold, 1975, 1980.

Barrett, Michele. *Women's Oppression Today: Problems in Marxist Feminist Analysis*. Thetford, Norfolk: The Thetford Press, 1985.

Benn, Connie. *The Developmental Approach: Demonstration Projects in the Brotherhood of St. Lawrence*. Sydney: University of New South Wales, Social Welfare Research Centre, 1981.

Blouin, Barbara. *Women and Children Last: Single Mothers on Welfare in Nova Scotia*. Halifax: Mount Saint Vincent University, Institute for the Study of Women, 1989.

Blum, Fred H. "Social Conscience and Social Values," in Irving Louis Horowitz, ed., *The New Sociology: Essays in Social Science and Social Theory in Honor of C. Wright Mills*. New York: Oxford University Press, 1964.

Braungart, Susan. "Social Workers out for New Standards," and "Social Workers plan Strike Vote," *Calgary Herald*, 1 April and 31 March 1989.

Bregha, Francis. *Public Participation in Planning, Policy and Program*. Toronto: Ministry of Community and Social Services, no date.

Bricker-Jenkins, Mary, and Nancy R. Hooyman, eds. *Not For Women Only: Social Work Practice for a Feminist Future*. Silver Spring, Md.: National Association of Social Workers, 1986.

Brook, Eve, and Anne Davis. *Women, The Family and Social Work*. London: Tavistock, 1985.

Brown, Chris. "Social Work Education as Empowerment," in Edna Chamberlain, ed., *Change and Continuity in Australian Social Work*. Melbourne: Longman Cheshire, 1988.

Buckley, Walter. *Sociology and Modern Systems Theory*. Englewood Cliffs, N.J.: Prentice-Hall, 1967.

Burns, Eveline. "Social Welfare is our Commitment," *Public Welfare*, 16, 3 (1958).

Cameron, Barbara. "Barriers to Success of Holistic Health," *Canadian Review of Social Policy*, 25 (May, 1990): 70-75.

Canada. Department of Indian Affairs and Northern Development. *Indian Child and Family Services in Canada. Final Report*. Ottawa, 1988.

Canada. Department of Indian Affairs and Northern Development. *Indian Child and Family Services Management Regime: Discussion Paper*. Ottawa, 1989.

Canada. House of Commons. Parliamentary Task Force on Program

Review (Nielsen Task Force). *Improved Program Delivery: Indians and Natives*. Ottawa: Supply and Services Canada, 1986.

Canadian Association of Social Workers. "Code of Ethics." Ottawa, 1983.

Canadian Child Welfare Association. *A Choice of Futures: Canada's Commitment to its Children*. Ottawa, 1989.

Carasco, Emily F. "Canadian Native Children: Have Child Welfare Laws Broken This Circle?" *Canadian Journal of Family Law*, 5 (1986): 111–38.

Carniol, Ben. *Case Critical: The Dilemma of Social Work in Canada*. Toronto: Between the Lines, 1987.

Carniol, Ben. *Case Critical: Challenging Social Welfare in Canada*. Toronto: Between the Lines, 1990.

Carniol, Ben. "Clash of Ideologies in Social Work Education," *Canadian Social Work Review* (1984): 184–200.

Carniol, Ben. "Democracy and Community Development in Canada," *Community Development Journal* (Oxford), 18, 3 (1983): 247–50.

Castellano, Marlene, Harvey Stalwick, and Fred Wien. "Native Social Work Education in Canada: Issues and Adaptations," *Canadian Social Work Review* (1986): 166–85.

Chambers, Clarke. *The Seedtime of Reform*. Minneapolis: University of Minnesota Press, 1963.

Chambers, Clarke. "An Historical Perspective on Political Action vs. Individualized Treatment," in *Current Issues in Social Work Seen in Historical Perspective*. New York: Council on Social Work Education, 1962.

Chandler, Robert. "The Profession of Social Work," in Joanne Turner and Francis Turner, eds., *Canadian Social Welfare*. Don Mills, Ont.: Collier-Macmillan, 1986.

Chock, Phyllis Pease, and June R. Wyman. *Discourses and the Social Life of Meaning*. Washington: Smithsonian Institute Press, 1986.

Clague, Michael, Robert Dill, Roop Seebaran, and Brian Wharf. *Reforming Human Services: The Experience of the Community Resource Boards in B.C.* Vancouver: University of British Columbia Press, 1986.

Clement, Wallace. *The Canadian Corporate Elite: An Analysis of Economic Power*. Toronto: McClelland and Stewart, 1975.

Clement, Wallace. *Class, Power and Property*. Toronto: Methuen, 1983.

Cleverdon, Catherine. *The Women's Suffrage Movement in Canada*. Toronto: University of Toronto Press, 1974.

Cochran, Moncrieff. "The Parental Empowerment Process: Building on Family Strengths," in J. Harris, ed., *Child Psychology in Action: Linking Research and Practice*. London: Croom Helm, 1985.

Conde, Carole, and Karl Beveridge. *First Contract: Women and the Fight to Unionize*. Toronto: Between the Lines, 1986.

Cook, R., and W. Mitchinson, eds. *The Proper Sphere: Women's Place in Canadian Society*. Toronto: Oxford University Press, 1976.

Corrigan, Paul, and Peter Leonard. *Social Work Practice Under Capitalism: A Marxist Approach*. London: Macmillan, 1978.

Cummings, Joan E. "Sexism in Social Work: Some Thoughts on Strategy for Structural Change," *Catalyst: A Socialist Journal of the Social Services*, No. 8 (1980).

Cummings, Joan E. "Sexism in Social Work: The Experience of Atlantic Social Work Women," *Atlantis*, 6, 2 (Spring, 1981): 62–79.

Davies, Bernard. "Towards a Personalist Framework for Radical Social Work Education," in Roy Bailey and Phil Lee, eds., *Theory and Practice in Social Work*. Oxford: Basil Blackwell, 1982.

Davin, N.F. "Report on Industrial Schools for Indians and Half-Breeds, to the Right Honourable Minister of the Interior." Ottawa, 14 March 1879. (Copy of printed report in Saskatchewan archives.)

De George, Richard and Fernando. *The Structuralists from Marx to Levi-Strauss*. Garden City, N.Y.: Doubleday, 1972.

Doern, Bruce. *Political Policy Making*. Montreal: The Private Planning Association, 1972.

Eichler, Margrit, and Marie Lavigne. "Women's Movement," in *The Canadian Encyclopedia*. Edmonton: Hurtig, 1985.

Ephross, Paul H., and Michael Reisch. "The Ideology of Some Social Work Texts," *Social Service Review*, 56 (June, 1982): 273–91.

Fabricant, Michael. "The Industrialization of Social Work Practice," *Social Work*, 30, 5 (1985): 389–402.

Falck, Hans S. *Social Work: The Membership Perspective*. New York: Springer Publishing, 1988.

Fanon, Franz. *The Wretched of the Earth*. New York: Grove Press, 1981.

Fay, Brian. *Social Theory and Political Practice*. London: George Allen and Unwin, 1975.

Fiddler, Sidney J. "Ethnic Competence: Social Work with Indian Minorities." M.S.W. thesis, University of Regina, 1988.

Findlay, Peter. "Critical Theory and Social Work Practice," *Catalyst*, No. 3 (1978): 53–68.

Fisher, Dena. "Problems for Social Work in a Strike Situation: Professional, Ethical and Value Considerations," *Social Work*, 32, 3 (May-June, 1987): 252–54.

Frager, Ruth. "No Proper Deal: Women Workers and the Canadian Labour Movement, 1870–1940," in Linda Briskin and Lynda Yanz, eds., *Union Sisters: Women in the Labour Movement*. Toronto: Women's Educational Press, 1983.

Fraser, Neil. "The Labour Movement in the Explanation of Social Service Growth: the United States and Britain," *Administration in Social Work*, 3, 3 (Fall, 1979): 301–12.

Freire, Paulo. "Argentina: Pedagogy of the Question," *LADOC*, XVI, 6 (1986): 22–29.

Freire, Paulo. *Education for Critical Consciousness*. New York: Seabury Press, 1973.

Freire, Paulo. *Pedagogy of the Oppressed*. New York: Continuum Publishing, 1985.

Freire, Paulo. *Politics of Education: Culture, Power and Liberation*. Granby, Mass.: Bergin and Garvey, 1985.

Galper, Jeffry. *The Politics of Social Services*. Englewood Cliffs, N.J.: Prentice-Hall, 1975.

Galper, Jeffry. *Social Work Practice: A Radical Perspective*. Englewood Cliffs, N.J.: Prentice-Hall, 1980.

Garbarino, James. "An Ecological Approach to Child Maltreatment," in Leroy Pelton, ed., *The Social Context of Child Neglect and Abuse*. New York: Human Sciences Press, 1981.

Germain, Carel B., ed. *Social Work Practice: People and Environments: An Ecological Perspective*. New York: Columbia University Press, 1980.

Germain, Carel, and Alex Gitterman. *The Life Model of Social Work Practice*. New York: Columbia University Press, 1980.

Giroux, Henry. "Education in Democracy and Empowerment," *Tikkun*, 3, 5 (1988): 30–33.

Giroux, Henry. *Theory and Resistance in Education*. Granby, Mass.: Bergin and Garvey, 1983.

Goldstein, Joan. "Bertha C. Reynolds – Gentle Radical." D.S.W. thesis, Yeshiva University, 1981.

Googins, Bradley, and Joline Godfrey. *Occupational Social Work*. Englewood Cliffs, N.J.: Prentice-Hall, 1987.

Gould, Ketayun. "Life Model Versus Conflict Model: A Feminist Perspective," *Social Work*, 32, 4 (1987): 346–51.

Greenspan, Miriam. *A New Approach to Women and Therapy*. Toronto: McGraw-Hill Ryerson, 1983.

Guest, Dennis. *The Emergence of Social Security in Canada*. Vancouver: University of British Columbia Press, 1980.

Gusfield, Joseph. *Protest, Reform and Revolt: A Reader in Social Movements*. New York: Wiley and Son, 1970.

Gutierrez, Gustavo. *The Power of the Poor in History*. New York: Orbis Books, 1983.

Halladay, Allan. "Confronting Disadvantage Within the Framework of

Social Justice," in Edna Chamberlain, ed., *Change and Continuity in Australian Social Work*. Melbourne: Longman Cheshire, 1988.

Halmos, Paul. *The Personal and the Political: Social Work and Political Action*. London: Hutchinson and Co., 1978.

Hartman, Ann, and Joan Laird. *Family-Centred Social Work Practice*. New York: The Free Press, 1983.

Hartsock, Nancy. "Feminist Theory and the Development of Revolutionary Strategy," in Zillah Eisenstein, ed., *Capitalist Patriarchy and the Case for Socialist Feminism*. New York: Monthly Review Press, 1979.

Havemann, Paul L. "Law, State and Indigenous People: Pacification by Coercion and Consent," in T.C. Caputo, M. Kennedy, C.E. Reasons, and A. Brannigan, eds., *Law and Society: A Structuralist Perspective*. Toronto: Harcourt Brace Jovanovich, 1989.

Havemann, Paul L. "The Indigenization of Social Control in Canada," in B. Morse and G. Woodman, eds., *Indigenous Law and the State*. Dordrecht, Holland: Foris Publications, 1988.

Havemann, Paul L. "The Over-Involvement of Indigenous People with the Criminal Justice System: Questions and Problem Solving," in Kayleen M. Hazelburst, ed., *Seminar Proceedings No. 7, Aboriginal Criminal Justice Workshop*. Canberra: Australian Institute of Criminology, 1985.

Hellman, John. *Simone Weil: An Introduction to Her Thought*. Waterloo, Ont.: Wilfrid Laurier University Press, 1982.

Hepworth, Dean H., and JoAnn Larsen. *Direct Social Work Practice: Theory and Skills*, 2nd edition. Homewood, Ill.: The Dorsey Press, 1986.

Heron, Craig. *The Canadian Labour Movement: A Short History*. Toronto: James Lorimer, 1989.

Hooks, Bell. *Feminist Theory: From Margin to Center*. Boston: South End Press, 1984.

Horowitz, Irving Louis, ed. *The New Sociology: Essays in Social Science and Social Theory in Honor of C. Wright Mills*. New York: Oxford University Press, 1964.

Howlett, Dennis. "Social Movement Coalitions – New Possibilities for Social Change," *Canadian Dimension*, 23, 8 (November-December, 1989): 41–47.

Hudson, Peter, and Brad MacKenzie. *Evaluation of the Dakota Ojibway Child and Family Services*. Prepared for the Dakota Ojibway Child and Family Services and the Evaluation Branch, Department of Indian Affairs and Northern Development, 1984.

Hurl, Lorna. "Privatized Social Service Systems: Lessons from Ontario's Children's Services," *Canadian Public Policy*, 10, 4 (December, 1984): 395–405.

Jacoby, Russell. *Social Amnesia: A Critique of Contemporary Psychology from Adler to Laing*. Boston: Beacon Press, 1975.

Jaggar, Alison. *Feminist Politics and Human Nature*. Totowa, N.J.: Rowman and Allanheld, 1983.

Jay, Martin. *The Dialectical Imagination*. Toronto: Little, Brown and Co., 1973.

Jenness, Dr. Diamond. *Plan for Liquidating Canada's Indian Problem Within 25 Years*. Report to the Special Joint Committee appointed to examine and consider the Indian Act. Ottawa, 1947.

Johnson, Louise C. *Social Work Practice: A Generalist Approach*. Boston: Allyn and Bacon, 1983.

Johnston, Patrick. *Native Children and the Child Welfare System*. Toronto: James Lorimer, 1983.

Jones, Frank. "NDP an idea that just didn't work," *Toronto Star*, 7 March 1989, p. F1.

Jordan, Bill. *The Identity of Social Work*. Occasional Paper No. 85. St. Lucia: University of Queensland, Department of Social Work, 1985.

Kealey, Gregory S. "The Structure of Canadian Working-Class History," in W.J.C. Cherwinski and G.S. Kealey, eds., *Lectures in Canadian Labour and Working Class History*. St. John's: Memorial University of Newfoundland, 1985.

Keefe, Thomas. "Empathy Skill and Critical Consciousness," *Social Casework*, 61, 7 (September, 1980): 387–93.

Kindervater, Suzanne. *Nonformal Education as an Empowering Process*. Amherst, Mass.: University of Massachusetts, Center for International Education, 1979.

Konopka, Gisela. *Eduard C. Lindeman and Social Work Philosophy*. Minneapolis: University of Minnesota Press, 1958.

Kramarae, Cheris, and Paula A. Treichler. *A Feminist Dictionary*. London: Pandora Press, 1985.

Kramer, R., and H. Sprecht. *Readings in Community Organization Practice*. Englewood Cliffs, N.J.: Prentice-Hall, 1983.

Kuhn, Thomas. *The Structure of Scientific Revolutions*. Cambridge: Cambridge University Press, 1962.

Kuper, Leo. *Genocide: Its Political Use in the Twentieth Century*. New Haven: Yale University Press, 1981.

Kuper, Leo. *International Action Against Genocide*. London: Minority Rights Group, Report No. 53, January, 1982.

Lane, Robert. "The Field of Community Organization," in *Proceedings of the National Conference of Social Work*. New York: Columbia University Press, 1939.

Langan, M. "The Unitary Approach: A Feminist Critique," in Eve Brook and Ann Davis, eds., *Women, the Family and Social Work*. London: Tavistock, 1985.

Lawrence, Kathleen. "Deepening Workers' Demands," paper for Labour Education, Ontario Institute for Studies in Education, 1986.

Lee, Bill. *The Pragmatics of Community Organization*. Mississauga, Ont.: Common Act Press, 1986.

Lee, Porter R. "Social Work: Cause and Function," in *Proceedings of the National Conference of Social Work 1929*. Chicago: University of Chicago Press, 1930.

Lem, Gail. "Helping hand may work best at arm's length" and "Program's primary purpose is to assist the worker," *Globe and Mail*, 3 January 1987, Section B, pp. 1, 3.

Leonard, Peter. "Towards a Paradigm for Radical Practice," in Roy Bailey and Mike Brake, eds., *Radical Social Work*. London: E. Arnold, 1975.

Levine, Helen. "Feminist Counselling – A Look at New Possibilities," *'76 and Beyond*. Special Issue of *The Social Worker*, 44 (1976): 12.

Levine, Helen. "The Personal Is Political: Feminism and the Helping Professions," in Angela Miles and Geraldine Finn, eds., *Feminism in Canada: From Pressure to Politics*. Montreal: Black Rose Books, 1982.

Levitt, Ken, and Brian Wharf, eds. *The Challenge of Child Welfare*. Vancouver: University of British Columbia Press, 1985.

Lichtman, Richard. *The Production of Desire: The Integration of Psychoanalysis into Marxist Theory*. New York: The Free Press, 1982.

Liffman, Michael. *Power for the Poor*. Sydney: George Allen and Unwin, 1978.

Lightman, Ernie. "Professionalization, Bureaucratization and Unionization in Social Work," *Social Service Review*, 56, 1 (March, 1982): 130–43.

Lindblom, Charles. *The Policy Making Process*. Englewood Cliffs, N.J.: Prentice-Hall, 1968.

Lipsky, Michael. *Street Level Bureaucracy*. New York: Russell Sage Foundation, 1980.

London-Edinburgh Weekend Return Group. *In and Against the State*. London: Pluto Press, 1979.

Longres, J., and E. MacLeod. "Consciousness Raising and Social Work Practice," *Social Casework*, 61, 5 (May, 1980): 267–76.

Lowe, Graham, and Herbert Northcott. *Under Pressure – A Study of Job Stress*. Toronto: Garamond, 1986.

Lowry, Louis. *An Assessment-Survey Report of Indigenous Social Work Literature on Social Work Methodology*. Boston: Boston University School of Social Work, 1988.

Lubove, Roy. *The Professional Altruist*. Cambridge, Mass.: Harvard University Press, 1965.

MacLeod, Linda. *Battered But Not Beaten: Preventing Wife Battering in Canada*. Ottawa: Canadian Advisory Council on the Status of Women, 1987.

MacLeod, Linda. *Wife Battering in Canada: The Vicious Circle*. Ottawa: Canadian Advisory Council on the Status of Women, 1980.

MacKenzie, Brad. "Decentralizing Child Welfare Services in Manitoba: An Assessment of Policy Implementation and Service Impacts," paper presented to the Fourth National Conference on Social Welfare Policy, Toronto, October, 1989.

Maguire, Patricia. *Doing Participatory Research: A Feminist Approach*. Amherst, Mass.: University of Massachusetts, Center for International Education, 1987.

Marchant, Helen. "Gender, Systems Thinking and Radical Social Work," in Helen Marchant and Betsy Wearing, eds., *Gender Reclaimed: Women in Social Work*. Sydney: Southwood Press, 1986.

Maslow, A. *Towards a Psychology of Being*. New York: Van Nostrand, 1968.

McInnis, Grace. *J.S. Woodsworth, A Man to Remember*. Toronto: Macmillan, 1953.

Merton, Robert. *On Theoretical Sociology: Five Essays Old and New*. New York: The Free Press, 1968.

Miles, Angela R., and Geraldine Finn, eds. *Feminism in Canada: From Pressure to Politics*. Montreal: Black Rose Books, 1982.

Miller, James. *"Democracy is in the Streets": From Port Huron to the Siege of Chicago*. New York: Simon & Schuster, 1987.

Mills, C. Wright. *The Sociological Imagination*. New York: Oxford University Press, 1959.

Mitchell, Juliet, and Ann Oakley, eds. *What is Feminism: A Re-examination*. New York: Pantheon Books, 1986.

Moore, Dorothy. "A Social History of New Scotland," paper presented at the Conference of the British Sociological Association, University of Edinburgh, March, 1988.

Moreau, Maurice. "Practice Implications of a Structural Approach to Social Work," *Journal of Progressive Human Services*, 1 (1990).

Moreau, Maurice. "A Structural Approach to Social Work Practice," *Canadian Journal of Social Work Education*, 5, 1 (1979): 78-94.

Moreau, Maurice. "Structural Social Work Practice: A Case Illustration," Université de Montréal, l'Ecole de service social, 1985.

Moreau, Maurice, and Lynne Leonard. *Empowerment Through a Structural Approach to Social Work: A Report From Practice*. Ottawa: Carleton University, 1989.

Morell, Carolyn. "Cause is Function: Toward a Feminist Model of Integration for Social Work," *Social Service Review*, 61, 1 (March, 1987): 146–55.

Morse, Bradford W. "Aboriginal Children and the Social Welfare State in Canada: An Overview," paper presented at the Second Conference on Provincial Welfare Policy, University of Calgary, 1–3 May 1985.

Morse, Bradford W. *Aboriginal Peoples and the Law: Indian, Métis and Inuit Rights in Canada*. Ottawa: Carleton University Press, 1989.

National Anti-Poverty Organization. "Corporate Canada seeks cuts in social spending," *NAPO News*, 24 (Winter, 1989): 2.

National Council of Welfare. *In the Best Interests of the Child*. Ottawa, 1979.

National Council of Welfare. *Poverty Profile*. Ottawa, 1988.

Native Council of Canada. "Report of the National Day on Native Child Care: Challenges into the 1990s," Winnipeg, 24 May 1989.

Newman, Paul. "Program Evaluation as a Reflection of Program Goals," in Ray Thomlison, ed., *Perspectives on Industrial Social Work Practice*. Ottawa: Family Service Association of Canada, 1983.

Nova Scotia. Department of Community Services. *Report of the Task Force on Family and Children's Services*. Halifax, 1987.

Nova Scotia Association of Social Workers. *How Will the Poor Survive? A Discussion Paper on the Current Social Assistance System in Nova Scotia*. Halifax, 1987.

Nova Scotia Nutrition Council. *How do the Poor Afford to Eat? An Examination of Social Assistance Food Rates in Nova Scotia*. Halifax, 1988.

O'Brien, Mary. *The Politics of Revolution*. London: Routledge and Kegan Paul, 1981.

Ombomsawin, Raymond. "Alternatives in Development and Education for Indigenous Communities in Canada," monograph published by Indian and Northern Affairs, Canada, Evaluation Directorate, July, 1986.

Osberg, Lars. "The Distribution of Wealth and Riches," in James Curtis *et al.*, eds., *Social Inequality in Canada: Patterns, Problems, Policies*. Scarborough, Ont.: Prentice-Hall, 1988.

Panitch, Leo, ed. *The Canadian State: Political Economy and Political Power*. Toronto: University of Toronto Press, 1977.

Panitch, Leo, and Donald Swartz. *The Assault on Trade Union Freedoms*. Toronto: Garamond, 1988.

Parsons, Talcott. *The Social System*. New York: The Free Press, 1951.

Pascal, Gillian. *Social Policy: A Feminist Analysis*. London: Tavistock, 1980.

Pearson, Geoffrey. *The Deviant Imagination: Psychiatry, Social Work and Social Change*. London: Macmillan, 1975.

Pemberton, Alec G., and Ralph E. Locke. "Knowledge, Order and Power in Social Work and Social Welfare," in Harold Throssel, ed., *Social Work: Radical Essays*. St. Lucia: University of Queensland Press, 1975.

Pennell, Joan. "Union Participation of Canadian and American Social Workers: Contrasts and Forecasts," *Social Service Review*, 61, 1 (March, 1987).

Peters, Thomas J., and Robert H. Waterman, Jr. *In Search of Excellence*. New York: Warner Books, 1982.

Pincus, Allen, and Anne Minahan. *Social Work Practice: Model and Method*. Itasca, Ill.: F.E. Peacock Publishers, 1973.

Piven, Frances Fox, and Richard A. Cloward. *Poor People's Movements: Why they Succeed, How They Fail*. New York: Vintage Books, 1979.

Porter, John. *The Vertical Mosaic: An Analysis of Social Class and Power in Canada*. Toronto: University of Toronto Press, 1965.

Prentice, Alison, *et al. Canadian Women: A History*. Toronto: Harcourt Brace Jovanovich, 1988.

Rahman, Muhammad Anisur. "The Theory and Practice of Participatory Action Research," in Orlando Fals Borda, ed., *The Challenge of Social Change*. New York: Sage Publications, 1985.

Rand, Justice I.C. *Canadian Law Reports*, 2150 (1958): 1251–53.

Rappaport, Julian. "Studies in Empowerment: Introduction to the Issue," *Prevention in Human Services*, 3, 2/3 (November, 1984).

Rappaport, Julian, Carolyn Swift, and Robert Hess, eds. "Studies in Empowerment: Steps Toward Understanding and Action," Vol. 3, Nos. 2/3, *Prevention in Human Services*. New York: The Haworth Press, 1984.

Red Collective. *The Politics of Sexuality in Capitalism*. London: Red Collective and Publications Distribution Co-op, 1978.

Reynolds, Bertha Capen. *Social Work and Social Living*. New York: Citadel Press, 1951.

Reynolds, Bertha Capen. *Uncharted Journey*. New York: Citadel Press, 1963.

Reynolds, Bertha Capen. "Whom Do Social Workers Serve?" *Social Work Today*, 2 (1935).

Rich, Adrienne. "Compulsory Heterosexuality and the Lesbian Experience," *Signs: A Journal of Women and Society*, 5, 4 (Summer, 1980): 631–60.

Rich, Adrienne. *Of Woman Born: Motherhood as Experience and Institution*. New York: W.W. Norton, 1986.

Richmond, Mary. "The Retail Method of Reform," in Joanna C. Colcord and R.Z.S. Mann, eds., *The Long View: Papers and Addresses by Mary Richmond*. New York: Russell Sage Foundation, 1930.

Riddington, Jillian. "Providing Services the Feminist Way," in Maureen FitzGerald *et al.*, eds., *Still Ain't Satisfied: Canadian Feminism Today*. Toronto: The Women's Press, 1982.

Robey, David, ed. *Structuralism*. Oxford: Clarendon Press, 1976.

Robinson, Virginia. "Psychiatric Social Work," *The Survey*, LII (1924).

Rogers, C.R. *Client-Centered Therapy*. Boston: Houghton Mifflin, 1951.

Rose, Stephen M. "Community Organizations: A Survival Strategy for Community-Based, Empowerment-Oriented Programs," *Journal of Sociology and Social Welfare*, XIII, 3 (1986): 491–506.

Ross, David P., and Richard Shillington. *The Canadian Fact Book on Poverty, 1989*. Ottawa: Canadian Council on Social Development, 1989.

Ross, Murray. *Community Organization: Theory and Practice*. Toronto: Harper & Brokers, 1955.

Rothman, Jack. "Three Models of Community Organization Practice," in F. Cox *et al.*, eds., *Strategies of Community Organization*. Second Edition. Itasca, Ill.: F.E. Peacock Publishers, 1970.

Russell, Mary. *Skills in Counselling Women – The Feminist Approach*. Springfield, Ill.: Charles C. Thomas, 1984.

Schore, Lee. "The Fremont Experience: A Counselling Program for Dislocated Workers," *International Journal of Mental Health*, 13, 12 (Spring-Summer, 1984): 154–68.

Schore, Lee. *Occupational Stress: A Union-Based Approach*. Oakland, California: The Institute for Labour and Mental Health, 1984.

Schur, E.M. *The Awareness Trap*. New York: Quadrangle, 1976.

Schwartz, Mary. "Sexism in the Social Work Curriculum," *Journal of Education for Social Work*, 9, 3 (1973): 65–70.

Schwartz, William. "Private Troubles and Public Issues: One Social Work Job or Two?" in Paul E. Weinberger, ed., *Perspectives on Social Welfare*, 2nd edition. New York: Macmillan, 1974.

Scott, Ann M. "First Nations and Child Welfare: Towards an Indigenous Model." M.S.W. thesis, McMaster University, 1988.

Shragge, Eric. "Foreword," in Frédéric Lesemann, *Services and Circuses: Community and the Welfare State*. Montreal: Black Rose Books, 1984.

Smith, Brenda, and Tina Smith. "For Love and Money: Women as Foster Mothers," *Affilia*, 5, 1 (1990).

Smith, Dorothy. *The Everyday World as Problematic: A Feminist Sociology*. Toronto: University of Toronto Press, 1987.

Stalwick, Harvey. *Searching for my Children and Now They are Home: Study Guide Two*. Regina: University of Regina, The Taking Control Project, Faculty of Social Work, Social Administration Unit, 1987.

Stalwick, Harvey. *What was Said: Study Guide One*. Regina: University of

Regina, The Taking Control Project, Faculty of Social Work, Social Administration Unit, 1986 (book and videotape).

Stanley Liz, and Sue Wise. *Breaking Out: Feminist Consciousness and Feminist Research*. London: Routledge and Kegan Paul, 1983.

Stephenson, Marylee. *Women in Canada*. Toronto: General Publishing, 1977.

Sweet, Lois. "Strikers say kids' welfare is at stake," *Toronto Star*, 23 June 1986, p. C1.

Tambor, Milton. "The Social Worker as Worker: A Union Perspective," *Administration in Social Work*, 3, 3 (Fall, 1979).

Tambor, Milton. "Unions and voluntary agencies," *Social Work*, 18, 4 (July, 1973): 41-47.

Teather, Lynne. "The Feminist Mosaic," in Gwen Matheson, ed., *Women in the Canadian Mosaic*. Toronto: Peter Martin Associates, 1976.

The Years Have Spoken. New York: privately published, 1988.

Titley, Brian E. *A Narrow Vision: Duncan Campbell Scott and the Administration of Indian Affairs in Canada*. Vancouver: University of British Columbia Press, 1986.

Tomlinson, John. "The History of Aboriginal Community Work," in Rosamund Thorpe and Judy Petruchenia, eds., *Community Work or Social Change? An Australian Perspective*. London: Routledge and Kegan Paul, 1985.

Trolander, Judith. *Professionalism and Social Change*. New York: Columbia University Press, 1987.

Tudiver, Neil. "Forestalling the Welfare State: The Establishment of Programmes of Corporate Welfare," in Allan Moscovitch and Jim Albert, eds., *The "Benevolent" State: The Growth of Welfare in Canada*. Toronto: Garamond Press, 1987.

Turner, Joan, and Lois Emery, eds. *Perspectives on Women in the 1980s*. Winnipeg: University of Manitoba Press, 1983.

Valentich, Mary. "Feminism and Social Work Practice," in Joanne C. Turner and Francis J. Turner, eds., *Social Work Treatment*. New York: The Free Press, 1979.

Van Den Bergh, Nan, and Lynn B. Cooper, eds. *Feminist Visions for Social Work*. Silver Spring, Md.: National Association of Social Workers, 1986.

Venne, Sharon H. "Treaty and Constitution in Canada: A View from Treaty Six," in Ward Churchill, ed., *Critical Issues in Native North America*. Copenhagen: International Work Group for Indigenous Affairs, Document No. 62, December 1988/January 1989.

von Bertalanffy, Ludwig. *General Systems Theory*. New York: George Brazelier, 1968.

Webb, David. "Social Work and Critical Consciousness: Rebuilding Orthodoxy," *Issues in Social Work Education*, 5, 2 (Winter, 1985): 89-102.

Webb, David. "Themes and Continuities in Radical and Traditional Social Work," *British Journal of Social Work*, 11 (1981): 143-58.

Wharf, Brian, ed. *Community Work in Canada*. Toronto: McClelland and Stewart, 1979.

Wharf, Brian. *From Initiation to Implementation: The Role of Line Staff in the Policy Making Process*. Victoria, B.C.: University of Victoria, School of Social Work, 1984.

Wharf, Brian. "Toward a Leadership Role in Human Services: The Case for Rural Communities," *The Social Worker*, 53, 1 (1985): 14-20.

Wilson, Elizabeth. *Women and the Welfare State*. London: Tavistock, 1977.

Wilson, Elizabeth. "Feminism and Social Work," in Roy Bailey and Mike Brake, eds., *Radical Social Work and Practice*. London: E. Arnold, 1980.

Wilson, S.J. *Women, The Family and The Economy*, 2nd ed. Toronto: McGraw-Hill Ryerson, 1986.

Withhorn, Ann. *Serving The People: Social Services and Social Change*. New York: Columbia University Press, 1984.

Index

Index